Open and Distance Learning
Global Challenges

Open and Distance Learning
Global Challenges

Hemlata Talesra

AUTHORSPRESS

Worldwide Circulation through Authorspress Global Network
First Published 2004
by Authorspress

E-35/103, Jawahar Park
Laxmi Nagar, Delhi-110 092

e-mail: authorspress@yahoo.com
quantum_soul@mantramail.com

Typeset in NewCenturySchlbk by Chitra Computers

Open and Distance Learning: Global Challenges
ISBN 81-7273-158-2

Printed in India at Tarun Offset, Delhi.

Preface

The term 'open and distance learning' represents approaches that focus on opening access to education and training provision, freeing learners from the constraints of time and place, and offering flexible learning opportunities to individuals and groups of learners. Open and distance learning is one of the most rapidly growing fields of education, and its potential impact on all education delivery systems has been greatly accentuated through the development of internet-based information technologies, and in particular the world wide web.

Strongly linked with developments in information and communication technologies, open and distance learning has the potential to generate new patterns of teaching and learning. There is evidence that it can lead to innovation in mainstream education, and may even have effects beyond the realm of education itself. Therefore, it plays an especially decisive role in the creation of the global knowledge-based society.

In this globalised age, it is more than ever clear that open and distance learning will be an important element of future education and training systems. It is approaching acceptance within mainstream education and training in such a way that it will make up part of the repertoire of most educational institutions in the future. Furthermore, there is a significant trend towards intensifying globalisation. Institutional and inter-governmental cooperation is increasing, and the 'global classroom' has been realised in quite a number of projects, particularly in connection with emerging global communications networks.

Faced with new training demands and new competitive challenges, more and more traditional universities are rapidly transforming themselves from single mode to dual mode universities, recognising the importance of distance education in providing students with the best and most uptodate educational resources available, in addition to the traditional teaching methods that they receive. The increasing number of open universities being established across the world is highly indicative of this trend. As governments are become more aware of the potential of open and distance learning, it is essential for their educational planning that the opportunities offered by new technologies be realistically examined within the framework of national development plans in general, and educational policies in particular.

The present book aims to review open and distance learning in the context of present challenges and opportunities, describe relevant concept and contributions, and outline some significant current global and regional trends. It is addressed to a wide range of audience, such as governments, governmental and non-governmental organisations, specialised institutions, associations, policy makers, teachers, students and others interested in this field, to help them in meeting today's urgent needs of education and training through open and distance learning.

Editor

Contents

1

The Potentials of Open and Distance Learning

The term 'open and distance learning' represents approaches that focus on opening access to education and training provision, freeing learners from the constraints of time and place, and offering flexible learning opportunities to individuals and groups of learners. In this educational process all most of the teaching is conducted by someone removed in space and/or time from the learner, with the effect that all or most of the communication between teachers and learners is through an artificial medium, either electronic or print. By definition, in open and distance learning, the normal or principal means of communication is through technology. Obviously teachers in conventional classrooms may use technology as a supplement to their teaching, but since it is not their principal means of communication the classroom is not considered to be open and distance learning. Another way of discriminating between distance and other forms of education is to ask where the principal educational decisions are made.

The rationale for open and distance learning (ODL) from its earliest days has been to open opportunity for learners to study regardless of geographic, socioeconomic or other constraints. The use of the term open is intended to highlight this key feature of the theory and practice of distance education. The open nature of education that is mediated by electronic or printed technologies might be formally institutionalised in such policies as open admissions, freedom of selection of what, when and where to learn. ODL organisations may indeed limit the extent of their openness, but traditionally they have shown a strong bias towards supporting the freedom of individual learners to exercise choice over one or more of the main processes of their learning. Typically this involves helping learners take responsibility for aspects such as what they learn, how they learn, where they learn, how quickly they learn, who to turn to for help and whether, when and where to have their learning assessed.

ODL is usually contrasted with conventional or face-to-face education, which may be described as the form of education which takes place in a classroom or an auditorium. However, both distance and face-to-face education are labels covering a wide range of variations and methods. Face-to-face education may vary along a continuum from one-to-one tutorials, group activities, seminars and classroom teaching to lectures for large audiences. In each case different educational philosophies may be applied and different methods may be used.

Face-to-face education may be supported by a range of media, and may be combined with periods of independent study. In a similar way, ODL has a variety of forms, according to the underlying educational philosophy, organisational approach and choice of technology, and distance educators may incorporate into their programmes an element of face-to-face teaching.

The evolution of ODL has been in four main phases, each with its own organisational form derived from the main form of communication.

i) *Correspondence systems* originated at the end of the nineteenth century, and are still the most widely used form of ODL in less developed countries. Based around a study guide in printed text and often accompanied by audio and video components such as records and slides, interaction in the correspondence method is by letters and other written or printed documents sent through postal systems.

ii) *Educational television and radio systems* use various delivery technologies —terrestrial, satellite, and cable television and radio — to deliver live or recorded lectures to both individual home-based learners and groups of learners in remote classrooms where some face-to-face support might be provided. Some systems offered limited audio or videoconferencing links back to the lecturer or a moderator at a central point.

iii) *Multimedia systems* encompass text, audio, video, and computer-based materials, and usually some face-to-face learner support delivered to both individuals and groups. In this approach, which is that used by the open universities, instruction is no longer an individual's work, but the work of teams of specialists, media specialists, information specialists, instructional design specialists, and learning specialists. Programmes are prepared for distribution over large numbers of learners, usually located across a whole country.

iv) *Internet-based systems* in which multimedia (text, audio, video and computer-based) materials in electronic format are delivered to individuals through computers, along with access to databases and electronic libraries, and which enable teacher-student and student-student, one-to-one, one-to-many, and many-to-many interactions, synchronously or asynchronously, through e-mail, computer conferences, bulletin boards, etc.

The earliest form of distance learning took place through correspondence courses in Europe. This was the accepted norm until the middle of this century, when instructional radio and television became popular. In the late 1950s and early 1960s, television production technology was largely confined to studios and live broadcasts, in which master teachers conducted widely-broadcast classes. Unfortunately, teachers who were expert in the subject matter were not necessarily the best and most captivating television talent, nor was the dull "talking head" medium the best production method for holding the interest of the audience.

In the early 1970s, the emphasis turned from bringing master teachers into the classroom to taking children out of the classroom into the outside world. This had the negative effect of relegating television to the position of enrichment, which was not perceived as really related to school work. This trend was reversed later in the 1970s, as professionally designed and produced television series introduced students to new subject matter that was not being currently taught, yet was considered to be an important complement to the classroom curriculum. Then, in the 1980s, the pendulum swung back to the basics. The most recent trend has been one of multiculturalism, humanities, and world affairs.

As increasingly sophisticated interactive communications technologies became available, however, they were adopted by distance educators. Currently, the most popular media are computer-based communication including electronic mail (e-mail), bulletin board systems (BBS's), and internet; telephone-based audioconferencing; and videoconferencing with 1- or 2-way video and two-way audio via broadcast, cable, telephone, fibre optics, satellite, microwave, closed-circuit or low power television. Audiographic teleconferencing using slow scan or compressed video and FAX is a low-cost solution for transmitting visuals as well as audio. Mosaic, a graphical interface to the world wide web, has become popular.

Each region has developed its own form of ODL in accordance with local resources, target audience, and philosophy of the organisations which provide the instruction. Many institutions, both public and private, offer university courses for self-motivated individuals through independent study programmes. Students work on their own, with supplied course materials, print-based media and postal communication, some form of teleconferencing and/or electronic networking, and learner support from tutors and mentors via telephone or e-mail.

As previous generation of technologies like correspondence, broadcast and narrowcast audio and video, and multimedia systems, produced particular forms of distance learning organisation, the spread of broadband internet communication is stimulating new types of educational organisations and also stimulating rethinking about the effectiveness of the older ones.

The new technologies are being taken up with equal enthusiasm by open universities, correspondence schools, established dual model institutions and by those now converting to dual mode status, as well as by newly emerging single model, purely electronic universities. Single model institutions are those in which ODL is the sole mission, to which teachers and administrative staff are exclusively dedicated. Course development, instruction, evaluation and other educational processes are tailored to the distant learner. In dual model institutions there may be an administrative staff whose sole responsibilities are ODL, but usually it is the teachers of the parent body who provide the teaching.

There is some allowance for distance teaching methods in course design, instruction and evaluation and teachers may have some special training. The most common distance learning design process is the author-editor model; each course is based on a study guide prepared by a single course writer. Where the internet is available the study guide may be accessed online rather than in hard copy.

Distance learning consortia may generally consist of two or more distance learning institutions who share in either the design or delivery of programmes, or both. Firstly, in many countries teachers in conventional institutions are required to teach at a distance as a responsibility added to their normal duties. Teachers have little training in distance methods. Such programmes may not have their own administrative or learner support services and there are relatively low levels of tailoring of course design, instruction and evaluation to the distant learner. Secondly, non-traditional providers, including private profit-oriented new companies are entering the global market, selling educational services online, especially to adult learners in the labour force.

For-profit universities are able to raise money in stock offerings tied to their ODL programmes. Some for-profit online programmes are growing twice as fast as the dual mode institution's face-to-face programmes, attracting students from more than a score of different countries. Some traditional education institutions are responding to such competition by establishing their own for-profit affiliates, while corporations have established their own in-house systems to meet their own needs for just-in-time and just-enough education.

COMPONENTS OF ODL SYSTEMS

The mission of a distance learning system may be directed towards particular purposes, target groups, regions, sectors or levels of education and training, and driven by particular values and philosophies of learning and education. Teaching strategies and techniques may depend partly on the type of programme and the needs they are designed to meet, but they also depend on the educational philosophy and values of the particular system, and the educational characteristics and potential of the technologies used.

Comprehensive, well designed learning materials and resources are essential components in all distance learning systems. They may stimulate self-directed learning and thus influence the quality of the system as a whole. Design, development and production of materials are often considered as a sub-system in distance teaching organisations. Previously produced, existing materials, textbooks, software, etc., may be used but in most cases each programme benefits from having specifically designed learning materials. Communication between teachers and learners is another necessary component. Communication technologies distribute messages in text, still and moving images, and sound. Knowledge-generating messages may be communicated to large numbers of learners, either synchronously or asynchronously, pushed by broadcasting or accessed on demand through audio/video players or internet.

New internet devices make it possible for larger numbers of people to share a common learning experience, in real time, and enable an individual learner to have a unique personal interaction with a teacher or with another learner, no matter where located. These experiences, since they do not depend on physical access, can be of much higher quality than were possible before. They will increasingly be available on a common platform, as bandwidth limitations become less significant than at present. They allow the organisation of virtual groups, and in countries where access to the internet is common, this is the fastest growing approach to distance teaching.

In most single model institutions, support delivered locally is a common component. A letter, a telephone call or an e-mail message is of course delivered locally and is more likely to be the means of learner support in dual mode institutions. What is meant here is, however, support in a form that allows some kind of direct (face-to-face) interaction between the learner and a teacher or a mentor/facilitator. This component may be organised completely as face-to-face events, or in combination with communication at a distance. Local support is usually given in a study centre or resource centre.

The student and staff management subsystem is another essential component of a distance learning system, which comprises admission, allocation to courses and student services, administering the learning and teaching procedures, assignments and assessment, monitoring dropout and completion, and examinations. Staff may be contracted on a part-time basis or may be in the core faculty in the case of a dual mode institution, but in either case they have to be recruited, trained and monitored. A range of other experts with different qualifications is also needed, either as full-time staff or as external consultants: planners, instructional designers, developers and producers, researchers, media experts, marketing experts and administrative staff. Effective management and administration needs not only competent staff, but also well designed, efficient administrative systems and routines, planning and monitoring systems, budgetary and accounting systems, etc.

In the ODL system, housing and equipment requirements are very much differing from conventional education institutions. A single mode distance learning system has no residential students, and thus there is little need for classrooms, lecture theatres, etc., at the central location. Such facilities may be needed locally, and are often provided in cooperation with local institutions. At the central location there will be need for production facilities and storage capacity, although some decentralised production is also possible of essential components in all distance learning systems. In a dual mode institution these ODL facilities have to be accommodated alongside the space dedicated to the institution's primary mission. Finally, evaluation should be a component, in order to provide information relevant to the adjustment of the roles and operation of system components, and in order to secure their optimal contribution and development.

The success of any ODL institution, dual or single mode, is highly dependent on the efficiency and effectiveness of the monitoring and evaluation system, without which it may be impossible for administrators to be aware of problems in the system until the system itself breaks down.

THEORETICAL CONCEPTS OF ODL

The theoretical basis on which instructional models is based affects not only the way in which information is communicated to the student, but also the way in which the student makes sense and constructs new knowledge from the information which is presented. Currently, there are two opposing views which impact instructional design: symbol-processing and situated cognition.

Symbol Processing

Until recently, the dominant view has been the traditional, information processing approach, based on the concept of a computer performing formal operations on symbols. The key concept is that the teacher can transmit a fixed body of information to students via an external representation. She represents an abstract idea as a concrete image and then presents the image to the learner via a medium. The learner, in turn, perceives, decodes, and stores it. W. Horton modifies this approach by adding two additional factors: the student's context (environment, current situation, other sensory input) and mind (memories, associations, emotions, inference and reasoning, curiosity and interest) to the representation. The learner then develops his own image and uses it to construct new knowledge, in context, based on his own prior knowledge and abilities.

Situated Cognition

This approach is based on constructivist principles, in which a learner actively constructs an internal representation of knowledge by interacting with the material to be learned. According to this viewpoint, both social and physical interaction enter into both the definition of a problem and the construction of its solution. Neither the information to be learned, nor its symbolic description, is specified outside the process of inquiry and the conclusions that emerge from that process. To implement constructivism in a lesson, one must shift one's focus away from the traditional transmission model to one which is much more complex, interactive, and evolving.

Though these theories are totally different in nature, effective designers usually start with empirical knowledge:

objects, events, and practices which mirror the everyday environment of their designated learners. Then, with a firm theoretical grounding, they develop a presentation which enables learners to construct appropriate new knowledge by interacting with the instruction.

Desmond Keegan's Theory

In Desmond Keegan's theory of ODL, the distance learning system must artificially recreate the teaching-learning interaction and re-integrate it back into the instructional process. This is the basis of their Iowa Model: to offer to the distance learner an experience as much like traditional, face-to-face instruction, via intact classrooms and live, two-way audio-visual interaction. In contrast, the Norwegian Model has a long tradition of combining mediated distance teaching with local face-to-face teaching.

Role of the Distance Teacher

When, through the most effective choice of media, teachers can meet the distance students face-to-face, they become facilitators of learning, rather than communicators of a fixed body of information. The learning process proceeds as knowledge building among teachers and students. ODL systems now involve a high degree of interactivity between teacher and student, even in rural and isolated communities separated by perhaps thousands of miles. Distance learning allows students to hear and perhaps see teachers, as well as allow teachers to react to their students' comments and questions. Moreover, virtual learning communities can be formed, in which students and researchers throughout the world who are part of the same class or study group can contact one another at any time of the day or night to share observations, information, and expertise with one another.

Design Considerations

In designing effective distance instruction, one must consider not only the goals, needs, and characteristics of teachers and students, but also content requirements and technical constraints. If unusual delivery systems are required, they must be made accessible to all participants. Revision based on feedback from instructors, content specialists, and learners is an ongoing process. Provisions must be made for continually updating courses which depend on volatile information, to keep the subject matter current and relevant.

Interactivity

Successful ODL systems involve interactivity between teacher and students, between students and the learning environment, and among students themselves, as well as active learning in the classroom. Though students felt that the accessibility of distance learning courses far outweighs the lack of dialogue, there is still a considerable lack of dialogue in telecourses when compared to face-to-face classes. Interactivity takes many forms; it is not just limited to audio and video, nor solely to teacher-student interactions. It represents the connectivity the students feel with the distance teacher, the local teachers, aides, and facilitators, and their peers. The quality and integrity of the educational process depends upon sustained, two-way communication. Without connectivity, distance learning degenerates into the old correspondence course model of independent study. The student becomes autonomous and isolated, procrastinates, and eventually drops out.

Active learning

As active participants in the learning process, students affect the manner in which they deal with the material to be learned. Learners must have a sense of ownership of the learning goals. They must be both willing and able to receive instructional messages. The mental effort which a learner will invest in a learning task depends on his own perception of two factors: the relevance of both the medium and the message which it contains ; his ability to make something meaningful out of the material presented. Television proved to be mentally less demanding than printed text when comparable content was employed. By giving students some expectations about the purpose of their viewing, he was able to influence the effort that students invested in processing the content of television instruction.

Visual imagery

Instructional television can motivate and captivate students, and stimulate an interest in the learning process. However, there are the unintended side effects of educational television in particular as well as "edutainment" in general. Reliance on exciting visuals may distort the curriculum by focusing students' attention on the entertaining and provocative features of the presentation rather than encouraging thoughtful analysis of their underlying meaning. If complex issues are presented in short units, through powerful images which may occur in any order, the end result may be oversimplification and superficiality. Students must learn to discriminate between "junk" information and quality information, to judge its reliability or bias, to identify distortions and sensationalism, to distinguish facts from persuasion, and to understand how the technology itself shapes the information it carries.

Effective communication

All instructional designers should begin with an understanding of their intended users, and to recognise them as individuals whose outlook is different from the designer's own. The golden rule for designers of instructional visuals is that "communicate unto others as they would communicate unto themselves". In other words, if you want the learner to construct an idea which is similar to yours, then use an image for your presentation which will trigger a similar idea in the learner's mind, in the context of the learning environment and the learner's prior experiences. No two learners will form the same idea, nor is it likely that their idea will be the same as that of the designer. How can this problem be solved? The key to good instructional design lies in the image presented. To quote Marshall McLuhan, "the medium is the message". It is up to the designer to use advance organisers to create an appropriate context for instruction and select effective images, using appropriate objects with relevant attributes, that will convey the same idea to the user as they did to the designer.

INSTRUCTION DELIVERING STRATEGIES

Teachers need training in instructional message design, strategies for delivering instruction on-camera, methods of diversifying types of presentation, selecting various mixes of student-teacher activities and interactions, choosing situations and examples which are relevant to their students, and assessing the level of learning by distant students. They also need plenty of guided, hands-on practice developing and delivering courseware using audio, full-motion video, graphics, and text, in front of a live audience, yet still in a non-threatening situation.

Strategies such as using fewer overheads and more moving video, interspersing "talking heads" with videos of sites, using hands-on experiments, incorporating text and graphic art, and other guidelines for effective video production are also valuable. Site facilitators, too, benefit from training programmes which emphasise hands-on practice with the equipment they are expected to use. Those who had participated in structured training programmes felt comfortable using the equipment, were able to engage their students in the learning process, and had mastered classroom management in a high-tech classroom.

Foreign language instruction presents special instructional challenges, not only because of the lack of immediate two-way interaction that characterises many ODL programmes, but also because of the loss of visual detail in videoconferences due to signal compression—especially detailed lip movements. This can be overcome by providing students with oral practice and feedback through telephone conversations with the instructor, and by instructional strategies that encourage frequent student-teacher and teacher-student dialogue.

Effective distance learning requires extensive preparation, as well as adapting traditional teaching strategies to a new learning environment which often lacks visual cues. Students must quickly become aware of and be comfortable with new patterns of communication, learn to manage their time, and take responsibility for their own learning. Teachers must enable students to establish contact with them, as well as interact among themselves. Site facilitators can act as the on-site "eyes" and "ears" of the teacher, stimulating interaction when distant students are hesitant to ask questions or participate in discussions.

The strategies which are effective in distance learning include: developing appropriate methods of feedback and reinforcement, optimising content and pace, adapting to different student learning styles, using case studies and examples which are relevant to the target audience, being concise, supplementing courseware with print information, and personalising instruction.

The variety of the available media presents a formidable research problem. One cannot compare print-based independent study courses, electronic projects on the internet, classroom BBS postings, audioconferences, and live, two-way interactive television, and expect that these comparisons will be valid. To add to this dilemma, media selection is often a question of media assignment. Teachers and site facilitators need training in those technologies which they are expected to use. More experimental studies are needed in the area of media selection, where researchers can compare the effectiveness of different technologies which deliver similar content to similar audiences.

Inquiry teaching promotes an environment that tolerates ambiguity and encourages students' questions. Teachers tended to ask the majority of the questions, rewarded students for guessing correctly, and required continual help in maintaining a classroom climate that emphasised reasoning rather than right answers. Only those teachers who had experience in inquiry-based instruction used the materials in open-ended ways. They found that it was important not only to provide training in the scientific concepts covered in the materials, but also to give participating teachers rich and varied suggestions for classroom activities .

Many distance educators have developed several inquiry learning modules. Collaborative groups of young distance learners participated in self-discovery activities, using manipulatives and conducting experiments under the guidance of the site facilitator, and then discussed their experiences with the studio teacher. Evidence of success is shown in the PMN video series (Pacific Mountain Network) through the enthusiastic responses of both teachers and students during and after the instructional sessions.

Progressive teachers who are early adapters of technology can become change agents for their peers. They can support other teachers by planning ahead as a group, and by working with the learning modules and equipment before using them in the classroom. Facilitators can try out learning modules as videotapes, building in interactivity as it suits the learning styles of their particular students, and then integrate real-time satellite programmes into their schedule later on. Technology providers, too, are available to answer questions from new users. The Satellite Educational Resource Consortium (SERC), for example, provides a contact person who visits the site, answers telephone calls, or provides printed support material. Studio teachers are available between sessions to reply to FAX messages or telephone calls.

The process of adapting new learning resources to the classroom, such as instructional television and videoconferencing, is not immediately transparent. Administrators cannot expect teachers to feel comfortable with the technology, to use it effectively, and to maintain it as well, without giving them extra resources and time. Instructors need access to data links and e-mail, as well as video links. They need to download and upload resources and lesson plans, consult with other teachers, and try out new learning modules.

MODES OF LEARNING

ODL systems were originally developed at the post-secondary level, and are only recently being used at the K-12 level. Adult learners have a wide variety of reasons for pursuing learning at a distance: constraints of time, distance, and finances, the opportunity to take courses or hear outside speakers who would otherwise be unavailable, and the ability to come in contact with other students from different social, cultural, economic, and experiential backgrounds. As a result, they gain not only new knowledge but also new social skills, including the ability to communicate and collaborate with widely dispersed colleagues and peers whom they may never have seen.

For effective distance learning, the preference of the student for a particular mode of learning, i.e., cooperative, competitive, or individualised is very important. Many current ODL projects incorporate cooperative learning, collaborative projects, and interactivity within groups of students as well as between sites. Some projects accomplish knowledge-building through student-initiated interactions and reflections, in real-time in class, and in delayed-time using an electronic bulletin board system (BBS). Some multimedia learning environments involve a dialectical opposition between the symbol-processing and constructivist viewpoints, to enable students to construct and transform knowledge through progressive discourse.

However, effective learning requires both knowledge of learner styles and advance preparation on the part of the teacher or site facilitator. Teachers and site facilitators are better able to make curriculum decisions to suit the preferences of their students, such as grouping certain students productively for project work, or assigning particular students to individual research projects, if they can determine the prevalent learning modes within their own classrooms. Site facilitators have the advantage of eye-to-eye contact and personal contact with students in their classrooms, whereas studio teachers must often rely on televised images, telephone conversations, or electronic messaging for feedback on student preferences. If a teacher recognises the existence of these alternate learning styles, and if he attempts to make a match between these modes and the content to be learned, then he can develop a local instructional theory. A localised theory has a greater prospect of success than a general instructional theory intended to function satisfactorily in variety of settings, with a variety of practitioners.

Student characteristics such as active listening and the ability to work independently in the absence of a live instructor become crucial for the success of a distance learning process. In a study Bernt and Bugbee examined two types of study strategies used by distance students: primary, cognitive strategies, such as the active listening, and secondary, affective strategies, such as ability to work independently of the instructor. The researchers found that students who passed their courses differed significantly in primary strategies from those who failed: in testwiseness, concentration, and time management skills. They found little difference among them in secondary strategies: active learning, diligence, and positive attitude.

Instructors tend to blame the high dropout rate among post-secondary students on poor time management and procrastination. However, miscommunication between students and teachers, and lack of course relevance to students, may also have negative repercussions. Teacher mediation increases the completion rate for ODL courses. Neither can we assume that all students have sharpened their primary study skills to the same extent, nor that a positive attitude will make the difference between success and failure. Students need support and direction to enable them to make the transition from traditional classroom environments to self-directed learning.

There are many ways of facilitating learner support. Studio teachers may visit the distant site, or students may take a trip to the studio. Audio and video teleconferences or interactive chats with mentors and other students are two real-time alternatives to site visitation, office hours or telephone calls. Interaction and support may also take place by delayed time. Students may e-mail or FAX questions to their instructors or fellow students, or post them on electronic BBSs. Teachers and peers, in turn, may respond at their convenience.

Frequent teacher-student interaction enables the teachers to get to know the students better than if their only contact were via a televised image from a distant classroom. Students, too, need guidance in putting information together, reaching their tutors, completing and submitting assignments, and charting their progress. Teachers also need support when they are learning about new technology, regardless of their level of classroom experience. As they begin their hands-on training with new technologies, some feel intimidated by the equipment, even in a non-threatening environment. At this point, they need to be able to communicate with other teachers who have gone through this process themselves, and who are competent to advise them and serve as role models. For example, the University of South Florida has set up a mentoring system and an online discussion for participants in the telecommunications course. The University of British Columbia uses teleconferences with other students and tutors, as well as a telephone tutoring system.

OPERATIONAL STRATEGIES

Planning, administration, management, and economics, all are crucial for a successful ODL programme. The roles of the teacher-facilitator-student triad, training of teachers and staff, implementation and adoption of new technology, and policy issues such as facilities, cost, and scheduling are also important.

Unlike in traditional education, distance learning teachers are not in direct classroom contact with their students. Communication is mediated not only by the technology, but also by a host of team partners which may include editors, designers, producers, technicians, media specialists, local tutors, aides, site facilitators, and service providers. Since many people must collaborate to produce and disseminate quality ODL programming, the need to plan and coordinate staff activity is essential. So that it is important to define the roles of the teacher and the site facilitator.

The distance learning teacher is the common thread throughout the distance learning process. He must be certified for the appropriate grade level, knowledgeable in his subject area, and trained in effective ODL strategies. He is responsible for knowing the subject matter, preparing lesson plans and producing an instructional module or course, selecting support materials, delivering the instruction effectively on-camera, determining the degree of student interaction, and selecting the form of distance evaluation or assessment.

A distance learning teacher must be better organised than an ordinary classroom teacher. He must be at ease with the equipment, and not let the technology get in the way of her presentation. This requires ongoing training in the form of regular observation of a master teacher, training in the use of carefully selected print, audio, graphics, and video materials, hands-on hardware training, and the chance to network with other teachers and facilitators on course progress. Currently, few teachers have had sufficient training or field experience to enable them either to be effective distant teachers or to use technology successfully in their classrooms. Proper training would help distance learning teachers to change their method of teaching and give more attention to advanced preparation, student interaction, visual materials, activities for independent study, and follow-up activities.

The new skills which teachers must learn as they assume the role of distance educators:

i) understanding the nature and philosophy of ODL
ii) identifying learner characteristics at distant sites
iii) designing and developing interactive courseware to suit each new technology
iv) adapting teaching strategies to deliver instruction at a distance
v) organising instructional resources in a format suitable for independent study
vi) training and practice in the use of telecommunications systems
vii) becoming involved in organisation, collaborative planning, and decision making
viii) evaluating student achievement, attitudes, and perceptions at distant sites
ix) dealing with copyright issues

A site facilitator's responsibilities are to motivate and encourage the remote site students, keep up their enthusiasm, and maintain discipline in the classroom. He is also responsible for the smooth running of equipment, helping students with interaction, handing out, collecting, and grading papers, guiding collaborative groups who are working with manipulatives, answering questions when necessary, and assisting the studio teacher when asked. He also carries out the assessment procedure defined by the teacher, via print, portfolios or online communications.

In general, site facilitators have an average of four classes, are mid-career staff rather than beginning teachers, are anxious about using new technology, and are selected by their principals because of their subject background, availability, and general teaching ability, rather than volunteering to be assigned as facilitators.

A number of concerns about instructional design and classroom management which were voiced by site facilitators, include:

i) facilitating vs. traditional teaching
ii) preparation
iii) timing and scheduling
iv) classroom logistics
v) other responsibilities.
vi) student misbehaviour and attitudes
vii) physical environment
viii) technical problems
ix) classroom dynamics

Classroom management, like technology expertise, is not a skill that is mastered once and for all by instructors in high-tech classrooms. They progress through a three-stage model of survival, mastery, and impact. It may take them at least two years to change their focus from being anxious about themselves, their new physical environment, equipment malfunctions, and student misbehaviour, to anticipating problems and developing alternate strategies, exploring software more aggressively, sharing ideas more freely, increasing student motivation and interest, and using technology to their advantage.

As classroom contexts change, so do classroom management issues. Educational change takes time, a great deal of support, and peer networking and guidance. In general, teachers tend to focus on the increased workload and drawbacks associated with an innovation before the benefits of change emerge and the innovation takes hold. Since their activities are closely related to those of the teacher, facilitators need similar training. However, some site facilitators perceive themselves as end users, rather than designers, of distance instruction, so they feel that they require less emphasis on instructional systems design.

Typical comments of site facilitators about the teaching/learning experience are that they have benefited from:

i) hands-on training and practice with assigned equipment
ii) a technical support team who can install, troubleshoot, and maintain classroom equipment and outside resources
iii) their own experiences anticipating equipment problems and working around them
iv) site visitation by studio teachers

TECHNOLOGY INTEGRATION

Maintaining appropriate equipment, and training teachers and facilitators to use it effectively, are necessary conditions, but are not sufficient in themselves to assure a school district of an excellent ODL programme. There are other factors involved, many of which are affective rather than cognitive, such as user-friendliness and the ability to implement learner support. School organisation has been traditionally hierarchical and bureaucratic, whereas new technologies challenge this model. Many teachers are slow to incorporate new technologies into their classrooms because they are now seen as workers, rather than as instructional leaders or motivating forces within their classrooms. On the other hand, the technological innovations that have been adopted by teachers are those which solved problems that the teachers themselves identified as important, regardless of outside change agents, the school administration, or the opinions of non-teachers. Successful technological innovations must take into consideration the social and political climate of the school, and must also reinforce the authority of the teacher, rather than undermine it.

The interrelated conditions must be met include:

i) training in the skills needed to work with technology
ii) education providing vision and understanding of state-of-the-art developments and applications
iii) support for experimentation and innovation
iv) sufficient time for learning and practice.
v) a shared vision of teaching and learning
vi) leadership and support for new technology from school administrators
vii) organisational conditions allowing flexibility, time, and incentives to experiment with new instructional methods
viii) opportunities for communication, interaction, and peer support among teachers
ix) training and personalised support over time for teachers.

A widely accepted technology is most often defined by a single characteristic: it makes a task rewarding for the user, where the "user" includes the student first, and the faculty second. If it does not make performance of a task rewarding, there is little motivation to accept the technology. Conversely, if it simplifies or expedites accomplishment of a goal, the probability of acceptance is high.

Teachers and facilitators adopt technology innovations in a hierarchy of needs, with the most basic needs generally being fulfilled before the higher ones. From basic needs to higher level ones, these are:

i) time and accessibility
ii) dependability
iii) ownership and authority
iv) control (influence on design)
v) integration.

Those site facilitators who believe in their own abilities to design instruction using satellite technology, and who are willing and able to continue in their role as teaching partners, have successfully incorporated technology into their classrooms. These site facilitators:

i) are committed to the concept of equality of education that satellite-based education provides.

ii) see opportunities for professional advancement through learning new skills and networking.

iii) seem revitalised by the observation of a master teacher and exceptional instructional design.

iv) realise that the programme will not work without their participation.

v) receive training in satellite-based instruction, either live or on tape, professional troubleshooting, and programme feedback.

The success is based upon a match between the identified needs of the facilitators and the resources which are available to them:

i) they are given time and accessible equipment.

ii) they are given assistance with equipment operation and troubleshooting.

iii) they take part in training and programme planning, and they control the grading classroom management, and classroom activities.

iv) they influence the programme through feedback.

v) they see the need for technology integration in order to take part in the programme.

MANAGING ODL

ODL changes the learning relationship from the common, centralised school model to a more decentralised, flexible model.

It also reverses social dynamics by bringing school to students, rather than students to school. This leads to a host of new issues for administrators to debate, including:

i) the impact of electronic education on tenured teaching
ii) balancing the budget with potentially low-cost electronic learning options
iii) redefining what it means to have a teacher present in the classroom
iv) revising teacher certification requirements to accommodate those teachers who electronically cross service area boundaries.

ODL enterprises are characterised by the integration of a great many parts working toward a common goal. Each school has its own aims, goals, and objectives, both stated and unstated. Each school also has its own culture, urban or rural, as well as its own perceived value of student learning. There are personnel issues, with clerical, technical, and educational support staff forming a vital link between teacher and student. Many facets of the project must be considered, especially linking student needs within the particular school district with current and projected technology resources. As opportunities arise, so do problems which must be dealt with.

A ODL delivery team requires well-trained individuals in addition to teachers, site facilitators, and administrators. Old roles are redefined, and new roles emerge. The principal or district administrator handles logistics, acquires equipment, and provides training and support. Some school districts have funds for a media specialist or technology coordinator. Certain technologies, like microwave videoconferencing, require a technician to run specialised equipment in a control room. Technical support staff install, maintain, and upgrade equipment. Clerical personnel process requests for equipment acquisition and repair, as well as reproduction and distribution of course material. Technologically astute students often assist teachers with new hardware and software and serve as peer tutors for slower students.

A development team should include subject matter experts, instructional designers, writers and editors, audio and video production staff, and curriculum developers. It is important to identify these "people resources", and assign appropriate tasks, responsibilities, and timelines, so that quality control can be maintained. Learning modules should be delivered on time to mesh with both the school schedule and that of the service provider.

One indicator of the need for distance learning teams to cooperate is the continuously rising costs of production. Sufficient money and time must be allocated to deliver whatever courseware was promised. Since funds come from the district, not from individual schools, ODL enterprises need to show a high degree of fiscal accountability. Although prices for technology are declining, taxpayers, school boards, and state legislatures, as well as both government and non-government funding agencies, expect to get the most for their funds. If money is short, then there are two options: either downsize the project or extend the timeframe.

Many proposals are written without regard for the time it takes to resolve development and delivery problems. People also require resources and time to build an effective team, to start and maintain the instructional development project, to develop a plan for formative evaluation, and to obtain a commitment on compensation issues. Once developed, the programme schedule may not fit in with the school schedule. Programmes may be too long, too short, or broadcast at the wrong time, resulting in a loss of real-time interactivity. One may always videotape the programme and show it later.

The cost/benefit of technology can vary significantly with the specific characteristics of schools and students. A successful programme in one location may be less successful elsewhere. While technology often improves educational quality, it is not necessarily cost-efficient. Teacher productivity can be raised only if the instructors behave as if they are in a virtual classroom, rather than deal with point-to-point or one-on-one communication situations. Though videoconferencing is effective, many classrooms lack access to dedicated telephone lines and modems, much less several thousand dollars worth of software and proprietary hardware.

CONTRIBUTIONS OF ODL

ODL is used for a wide range of purposes. It can be used at primary and secondary education levels to provide both in-school and out-of-school programmes. In-school ODL programmes are used to support teaching in schools when learning materials are lacking, or where enrichment is thought to be desirable. They may also be used where teachers do not have formal qualifications, or to support subjects where the number of pupils is too small to be able to organise conventional teaching.

A variety of approaches are used, including Interactive Radio Instruction (IRI), schools radio, educational television through terrestrial and satellite networks, multimedia schemes delivered through satellite, and web-based delivery of multimedia schemes. The materials may be designed for young children or for adolescents and adults.

ODL is used in out-of-school programmes both at primary and secondary level to educate school-age children and youth who are unable to attend ordinary schools, including those who are disabled, suffering from long-term illness, or living in remote areas or living outside their own countries. These programmes generally use correspondence methods. Some programmes are designed to provide lessons that parents can use to teach their own children. Other programmes are designed to be supported by teachers, with parents providing direct supervision. Such programmes may, for example, combine correspondence education with two-way radio contact. As well as focusing on isolated individuals, out-of-school programmes can also be directed at nomadic and itinerant groups. They may also be directed at youths and adults who dropped out of initial formal education, and for whom ODL represents a convenient opportunity at a later stage of their life.

Open schools, which use a variety of approaches (print, broadcast, face-to-face and other media), are of particular interest to high population countries. Those aimed at children offer the same curriculum as normal state schools: equivalency of standards and of qualifications offered is important to their legitimacy. Out-of-school programmes for adults tend to provide basic education through a range of models. Both radio schools and open schools targeting adults tend to provide a complementary—often vocational or socially-directed—curriculum.

In the non-formal and community development sectors of education, ODL has considerable effect. However, its potential has never been fully realised. Enthusiasm for basic adult education grew in the 1960s and 1970s just as technology began to be used more widely in education. Mass communication methods, often linked with some kind of group meetings and face-to-face support, were seen as one way of delivering a wide range of educational and skills programmes in support of agriculture, health and nutrition, political education, and development and employment-related projects, to large numbers of adults.

An early and influential prototype—the Canadian Farm Forums of the 1940s—suggested a way forward through the motto 'Read, listen, discuss, act'. This approach was later used in India and Ghana. Radio campaigns were another early and influential model. The idea was to deliver short, highly intensive campaigns to support major development ends. Research suggested, however, that audiences were often unresponsive, projects often inappropriate, and the lack of resources to follow up the campaigns meant that information cannot be turned into action with the result that campaigns of this kind were not repeated.

However, there is much anecdotal evidence of the effectiveness of small-scale non-formal education projects using radio—for example, to support health care in Sudan and rural women in Mongolia. Latterly radio and television dramas have been used in countries such as Gambia and Nigeria as a means of educating people about health issues such as family planning and HIV/AIDS. Indeed, radio in particular has a powerful role to play in non-formal education. Some of the early projects were designed to break free of those parts of the school syllabus that are irrelevant to adults, and instead offer a curriculum of more practical use to their audiences, but this thrust was not developed as much as it might have been in the face of economic findings that suggested that the case for investment in non-formal education was not as strong as that for investing in projects delivering the formal curriculum.

As a result the rapid development of non-formal education projects was curbed as enthusiasm for the idea that mass communication systems should be mobilised for development, and the financial resources that followed, began to wane. Nevertheless, the anecdotal evidence suggests that there are many successful but largely unreported and often formally unevaluated projects run by the extension services of ministries of health, agriculture, and labour, and by NGOs.

One relatively well reported project is the African Institute for Economic and Social Development (INADES), which operates as semi-autonomous efforts across eight francophone and two anglophone countries. It has done much to provide education aimed at farmers, agricultural extension agents, and women, using various approaches, including ODL. In Pakistan, the Allama Iqbal Open University provides non-formal education through its Functional Education Project in Rural Areas. Audiocassettes and flipcharts form a centrally produced resource for group leaders to use in discussion and study groups. Other university-based extension projects include the University of Namibia's action research pilot project on the use of affordable media for farmer education, which delivers information on best cattle husbandry practices to small-scale cattle farmers and the Yashwantrao Chavan Maharashtra Open University extension, community education and non-qualification programmes in India, which delivers programmes on agriculture, marital relations, personality development, ageing, child care, nutrition, first aid, vocational skills, and entrepreneurial development, to illiterate adults, new literates, less educated adults, leprosy patients, unemployed youths, etc.

Non-formal ODL projects are delivered through a vast range of organisational structures involving public community development services, popular movements and organisations, churches and religious organisations, charitable foundations and organisations, private institutions and government-funded schools, colleges and universities—but all in essence develop centrally produced materials that can then be used in distributed sites to deliver non-formal education locally to adults. The most common approaches involve print sometimes combined with correspondence teaching, some form of broadcasts or recorded media. The learners often come from the more marginalised sectors of society.

Non-formal education programmes have to be designed carefully to ensure that such learners can benefit from the programme. This requires a cadre of support workers. Generally learners enrol to achieve a particular learning objective, and wish to progress quickly. These characteristics determine the curricula, which are usually focused on specific issues to do with social and community education, health and family, and economic and earnings-related education, including agriculture. Moreover, projects can support equity goals—though this can be undermined by policies that require learners to pay for materials and services.

In the field of technical and vocational education ODL makes up a mixed and complex picture. It may include experimental work and hands-on training as an integral element. It has often been developed by private institutions and enterprises, and makes an important contribution to human development. It is often necessary to supplement distance learning with intensive experimental work and hands-on training through residential schools, home experiment kits, etc.

Electronically supported ODL programmes using the world wide web are now substantially employed in technical, vocational and professional education. Many countries have developed vocational, polytechnic and other types of short-cycle colleges, sometimes spanning both secondary and post-secondary levels. In this sector there are many examples of ODL programmes. In addition to management, business studies and technician training, one may also mention training for agriculture and for public administration and health services as important areas.

Continuing education and training is an expanding field in which ODL is used to a great extent. The need for recurrent and continuous updating of knowledge and skills is recognised as a fundamental demand in society today, and ODL with its decentralised and flexible delivery and its modular structure of courses and curricula has become an obvious way of meeting this need.

ODL institutions offer their courses and programmes for this purpose, and they are developing particular courses for particular needs. Cooperation and partnerships between enterprises, professional bodies and distance teaching institutions are growing, and consortia and special training institutions have been established in order to serve particular trades and professions with continuing education courses.

The National Technological University in USA offers one example, providing continuing education for engineers through satellite broadcasts from about 50 universities. The medical profession is another example of a profession which often uses ODL for continuing education purposes. Many large corporations also provide in-service training at a distance for their employees.

At the tertiary level of education, more distance learning courses are offered than at any other level. This has been the case since the invention of the ODL method near the end of the nineteenth century when the use of new technology made it possible to deliver higher education beyond the boundaries of the campus. The development of the open university in the United Kingdom provided the model for the integrated multimedia systems approach to the delivery of higher education by a single mode university, a model that has been emulated in more than a score of other countries. Open universities have their own degrees and curricula, though these are usually similar to the curricula and degrees of a conventional university. The similarity of curricula and degree structures may be seen as a demonstration of equal quality, and makes the recognition of ODL at the tertiary level easier.

The internet has attracted the attention of university academics to the idea of distance teaching in a way that no previous technology managed to do. Together with the pressure from new competitors for student enrolment, this enthusiasm for technology explains the growing number of traditional universities that are converting to dual mode status. Such universities usually teach the same curricula for distance students as for their residential students and subject the students to the same entrance requirements and examinations. The success and expansion of single mode open universities on the one hand, and the transformation of traditional universities to dual mode universities on the other, are important contributions to the diversification and development of higher education systems.

Teacher education is another important area where ODL has been used extensively to provide pre-service teacher preparation, upgrading of academic qualifications, and in-service continuing professional development in particular subjects, content areas and instructional methods. Many examples, particularly from both developing and developed countries, show that teacher training at a distance may reach large groups of teachers and may have profound impact on the development of national education systems.

The use of ODL for teacher education is a crucial strategy when expansion or quality improvement is needed in the public education system. Developed countries are using the internet as the principal or supplementary means of providing both pre-service and in-service teacher education. There is a growing number of high quality web-based professional development resources available for educators globally. The current and emerging communication and information technologies provide unique opportunities to continue the professional development of teachers and other educators. The web provides teachers with incredibly rich instructional and information resources to enhance their instruction and professional skills and the possibility of on-demand, just-in-time professional development without leaving their classrooms. It also provides opportunities for online mentoring and support of novice teachers during their first year of teaching and to develop online communities of practice.

ODL plays a major role in upgrading the knowledge and skills of teacher educators both in higher education and educational agencies. Web-based resources and tutorials may assist teaching faculty and teacher educators in upgrading their knowledge and skills in areas such as the new technology tools for learning in order that they may infuse and model the use of technology in the courses they offer to future teachers. A particular advantage of ODL is that it is makes teacher preparation and professional development programmes accessible to indigenous peoples and others located in remote, rural areas who do not have convenient access to higher education institutions and where there is often a shortage of well-prepared teachers and other educational professionals.

In many developing countries access to the web in local schools is not possible. However, the web may provide an important resource for teacher education institutions and agencies and centres that provide professional development to teachers in the country. In countries with limited access to technology infrastructure, radio, television and print-based materials are used to address teacher education needs.

ODL and the new tools for learning may serve as a catalyst for changing teaching practices, the roles of teachers and students as part of an overall strategy for systemic change of the educational system to reflect current knowledge on human learning and to help the educational system be more responsive to local and national needs as well as global trends.

GLOBAL INITIATIVES

Today, ODL is one of the most rapidly growing fields of education and training in the world. The potential impact of ODL on all education delivery systems, from primary to tertiary level, has been greatly accentuated through new developments in information and communication technologies, which increasingly free the learners from the constraints of time and space.

UNESCO is the specialised United Nations Agency with a mandate to provide education for all. During the last two decades the world has seen a considerable growth in education and training. But the world still suffers from intolerable inequalities both at the international level and within nations. Many countries are struggling with limited access to education and training for children and young people, and at the same time have to address basic needs of the older generation.

Low quality and insufficient relevance is a concern in many countries. At the root of most of these problems is the problem of financing an adequate provision of education and training. Some of the trends affecting education and training in most countries are: structural reforms in education and society; diversification of the resource base, privatisation, etc.; the fast development of information and communication technologies; the move towards a more knowledge-intensive economy; increasing integration and interdependence of world economy.

The potential of ODL in relation to some of the problems of education and training in the world today should be considered from different perspectives. For the student/learner it means liberation from the constraints of time and place, leading to the benefits of increased access and flexibility, as well as the combination of work and education. It may also mean enrichment and higher quality, and a more learner-centred approach with the possibility of new ways of interaction.

For employers it offers high quality and often cost-effective professional development and learning in the workplace. It allows upgrading of skills, increased productivity and development of a new learning culture. In addition, it means sharing of costs of training time and increased portability of training. For governments the main reasons for introducing ODL are its potential of increasing the capacity of education and training systems, reaching target groups with limited access to conventional education and training, supporting and enhancing the quality and relevance of existing educational structures, achieving more cost effective education and training, and promoting innovation and opportunities of lifelong learning.

While ODL designates various forms of mediated teaching and learning, characterised by the dispersion in time and/or space of learners and their teachers for the whole or parts of the study programme, open learning indicates a certain philosophy, underlining open entry and access to learning opportunities. Although there are no direct conceptual links between them, the two concepts are often used to describe similar types of educational provision, sharing a common inspiration of access to learning and flexibility of learning arrangements.

ODL and conventional education are labels covering a wide range of variations and methods. Very often methods from both forms are also combined. This means that although there may be a clear distinction in theory, the distinction between ODL and conventional education in practice is far from clear. Therefore, it is not very useful to look at ODL in isolation from other forms.

Distance learning systems always have several components, and it is important to be aware of components such as: mission, programmes and curricula, teaching/learning strategies and techniques, learning materials and resources, communication, interaction, support delivered locally, delivery system, students and tutors, staff and other experts, management and administration, housing and equipment, and evaluation.

ODL, like any other mode or approach, is not a panacea. Many of them are struggling with a range of problems and barriers to effective and successful implementation. Some of the more common obstacles and problems are: inadequate technological infrastructure, planning and programme deficiencies, lack of human capacity and expertise, inadequate economic resources; lack of recognition of educational equivalence, and neglect of learning conditions and cultural aspects. Sometimes ODL is used for school-age children and youth who are unable to attend ordinary schools, or to support teaching in schools, both at primary and secondary level.

However, most school equivalent courses and programmes are targeted towards the adult population. In developing countries, ODL for school equivalency is perhaps the only realistic way of expanding educational opportunities to the adult population. In the developed countries there is still a need for this type of programmes for those who missed out of the conventional system. Tertiary level ODL systems are also providing educational opportunities that are equivalent to conventional university and college education. Both private and public providers have made important contributions to the development of industry and trade.

Teacher training is a particularly important area. The teacher training includes both initial training for formal qualifications, in-service supplementary training for formal upgrading, and continuing in-service training in particular subjects and topics. Many examples, particularly from developing countries, show that teacher training at a distance may reach large groups of teachers and may have profound impact on the development of national education systems.

Community development and non-formal education are used in the ODL. ODL lends itself also to the teaching of many of the complex issues of the modern world, in which input from a variety of disciplines is necessary. It has the potential of generating new patterns of teaching and learning. Linked as it is with developments in information and communication technologies, it also is connected with the development of new learning needs and new patterns of information access and application. ODL therefore may lead to innovation in mainstream education, and may even have effects beyond the realm of education itself. The confidence is growing that ODL will be an important element of future education and training systems, and may offer some responses to the world's educational challenges.

ODL is approaching a state of acceptance within mainstream education and training that will in the future make it part of the repertoire of most educational institutions. The technological development allows for new patterns of access and delivery in education, often linked to new types of demands and new approaches to learning.

One of the trends is the emergence of new forms of distance learning based on more interactive telecommunication technologies, with implications of pedagogical, economic and organisational nature. There is a significant trend towards internationalisation. There is still limitation of access for a range of reasons, but the "global classroom" has already been demonstrated in quite a number of projects.

ODL has existed for about one hundred years in the more developed regions and for about one generation in the developing regions. In the developing world, ODL suffers from many of the same constraints and problems as education in general. In addition, lack of infrastructure and professional competence in ODL are important barriers. Nevertheless, these forms of education delivery have come to stay in the Third World, and many countries are looking at ODL as a major means of expanding education and training and increase the quality of education. Some countries have established major institutions—open schools and open universities—which seem to become cornerstones in their educational systems.

The needs of extending learning opportunities over the whole lifespan and the changing demands concerning knowledge and skills represent a challenge which is not easily met by conventional structures and institutions of education and training. New information and communication technologies seem to have great potential impact on education. Both existing ODL institutions and conventional institutions are eager to develop effective models of application of new technologies and at the same time meet the needs of learners, and do so with variable success.

A distance teaching institution needs to have sufficient resource to be able to react fast to meet new demands. There needs to be a planned, continuing interface between all the national stakeholders in ODL, in order to secure coordination. In many countries, international and regional bodies may have a role supporting and guiding developments at national level. One of the major contributions of ODL in developing countries is within teacher training. It has also contributed towards the improvement and expansion of basic schooling for youth and adults. In many developing countries ODL is a very important means of providing higher education. Its role in non-formal education is also well known. It is playing an important role in qualifying and upgrading key personnel.

Institutions of ODL often serve as resource centres for community-based learning, and provide an infrastructure for production and distribution of learning materials. There are, however, some common stumbling blocks for the effective implementation of ODL in developing countries. The lack of funding ad problems of sustained support are perhaps the most important ones, having detrimental effects on quality and achievements.

Another common problem is lack of human resources with sufficient competence and motivation. The third major problem is technological infrastructure, which prevents the effective use of appropriate technologies. Finally, the lack of strategic planning and coordination may reduce the level of achievement and cost effectiveness. Important strategies for future development should include harmonisation of goals, policy clarification and coordination at the national level, as well as regional coordination and collaboration.

Capacity building is also important, including increased professionalism in planning and management of ODL systems. Technology is in itself a driving force, which should be used for the benefit of education. The technologies used are not an end in themselves. They are used to extend the opportunities of learning to new groups, to make learning more efficient and flexible, and to enrich the learning processes. The potential of advanced technologies is linked to the capacity of storing, retrieving, manipulating and distributing large amounts of information, and of speeding up and facilitating communication.

The challenge will be to utilise this potential according to clear educational and instructional strategies, and to integrate the cultural and conceptual developments caused by the new technologies. Most of the successes of electronic information technologies so far have been in specialised or higher education. One of the major weaknesses has been in facilitating basic education.

The developing countries have benefited the least from the potential of educational technology. Interactivity is a key element of most of the new services foreseen. They are particularly adapted to education and to the communication need of dispersed users, but on the other hand need reliable networks. For electronic information technologies to be successfully employed in education on a wide scale, major changes will have to be introduced into education systems.

New technologies in education imply new relationships between learners and the available information as the learners acquire knowledge and build knowledge structures. The education sector should probably organise itself as a major technology customer and partner in service development, although not necessarily as producer of learning materials.

Without doubt, ODL will be adapted and integrated by "conventional" institutions, probably at all levels and in all sectors. New markets and new technologies will impose changes in these institutions as well, and new types of institutions and services will be established. Existing institutions will need to develop new types of partnerships and alliances in order to meet the needs of society in more effective ways than most of them do today. The wealth of experience and competence in existing ODL institutions must be capitalised in new alliances and structures.

ODL is cheaper than other forms of education and training. Usually, the cost structure in ODL is quite different from cost structures in conventional types of education. Clearly, when capital investments substitute high recurrent costs, as is often the case in this field, there is an important factor in the economy of scale.

While conventional education and training show great variation in costs according to subject area and type of programme, ODL also varies very much according to use of learning materials, other media and technologies, and types and organisation of student support services.

The funding of ODL institutions is different from that of conventional institutions. On the other hand, if ODL is to be used increasingly by conventional institutions, funding for programmes of this type needs some harmonisation with funding mechanisms for conventional programmes. The students in ODL, who are often working adults, should pay a higher proportion of the costs than conventional students do. As ODL becomes a regular feature in the education system, care should be taken to remedy any unjustified economic discrimination between groups of students.

The importance of ODL has dramatically accentuated as a result of rapid population growth and development trends, which called for more effective systems of educational delivery.

Parallelly, however, new chances to cope with the situation became available through an unforeseen development of information and communication technologies.

Facing the educational challenges of the twenty-first century, UNESCO has planned to strengthen its contribution to the development of ODL. It will accomplish through the functions of advocacy, clearing-house, capacity-building and cooperation. The advocacy function consists of generating public interest in the use of innovative ODL methods; sensitising national policy and decision makers to the potentials of these methods to meet the educational needs; facilitating the collaboration of international, regional and subregional networks in the field and enhancing their partnership with information, communication, industrial and other related sectors.

The clearing-house function assigns UNESCO an important "observatory" role in promoting international cooperation for monitoring and inventorying present and future open and ODL activities; collecting, processing and disseminating relevant information and experience to member states and other partners concerned, and strengthening the cooperation with existing information centres and specialised agencies, and assisting governments to establish relevant data bases in this field. The capacity-building function refers to the Organisation's efforts of assisting its member states in developing their ODL systems through a wide range of activities, such as establishing policies and priorities; setting up delivery systems, institutes and programmes; improving management, administration and student support systems; promoting material and course production; intensifying the training of personnel; extending the use of information and communication technologies.

REFERENCES

Bates A.W., *Technology, Open Learning and Distance Education*, London: Routledge, 1995.

Barron, A., and G. Orwig, *New Technologies for Education*, Englewood, CO: Libraries, 1993.

Dalit, Jessica, "The Policy Context of Open and Distance Learning", *Journal of Open and Distance Learning,* PUP 2000.

Eager M., "Distance education: The indicators", *People Dynamics*, 13(2), January, pp. 17-20, 1996.

Evans, T. and D. Nation, "Education within and without classrooms: Sustaining quality through technological change", In A. Tait, (ed.): *Quality Assurance in Open and Distance Learning—European and International Perspectives*, Cambridge: The Open University, 1993.

Garrison, D.R., and D. Shale, "Mapping the boundaries of distance education: Problems in defining the field", *The American Journal of Distance Education*, 1(1), 7-13, 1987.

Keegan, D., *The Foundations of Distance Education*, London: Croom Helm, 1986.

Moore, Michael M. and Alan Tait, "Open and Distance Learning: Trends Policy and Strategy Considerations", *Division of Higher Education*, UNESCO, 2002.

Perraton, H., "A theory for distance education", In D. Sewart, D. Keegan, and B. Holmberg (eds.), *Distance education: International Perspectives,* New York: Routledge, 1988, pp. 34-45.

Schamber, L., "Delivery systems for distance education", *ERIC Document Reproduction Service* No. ED 304 111, 1988.

Schlosser, C.A., and M.L. Anderson, *Distance Education: Review of the Literature*, Washington, DC: Association for Educational Communications and Technology, 1994.

2

Impacts of ICTs in Open and Distance Learning

Digitisation and the convergence of computer and telecommunications have led to a range of information and communication technologies (ICT); they are transforming tertiary education. Within open and distance learning (ODL) systems, technologies are used for two contrasting purposes: to distribute teaching material and to stimulate learning by means of one-way or two-way communication. An appropriate technology needs to be found to distribute material to students. In the case of physical teaching material, such as books or audio cassettes, material has to be carried direct to students or to a point from which they can collect it. It may be possible to use existing channels of communication with teachers for this purpose, or to rely on the post, or to set up a dedicated service. Broadcasting, by radio or television, videoconferencing and computer communication all offer means of delivering teaching material to learners without these physical arrangements. Teaching involves more than distribution. Well-designed printed materials, cassettes, or broadcasts are usually designed to promote learning, often by stimulating an active response from the learner.

In choosing technologies, the policy maker has to consider not just how materials will be distributed but how they can be designed to facilitate learning and to resolve tensions between these two aims. Television, for example, may look the best medium for showing a simulation in engineering but is inappropriate if the only available television hours are at an inconvenient time or on a channel which does not reach most of the learners. If ODL is to involve more than providing resources to teachers, it also demands two-way communication. This may be immediate, in the case of telephone tutoring or videoconferencing with a two-way audio circuit, or delayed, typically through the use of written assignments.

New technologies are reducing the lengths of the delays here: it is sometimes possible for learners to send assignments to a tutor by fax or email. Two-way communication is also possible, of course, through face-to-face contact. In making decisions about technologies we need to consider not just those that are mediated but also the role of face-to-face contact if this is part of the distance-education system we are creating. Thus, the planner's decisions are usually about a set of technologies, chosen according to their appropriateness for the subject matter and the audience, and to their cost.

In ODL we may use print to present material, the mail to distribute it, and face-to-face tutorial sessions for feedback and dialogue. Planners are likely to be able to choose between some or all of these technologies. Print remains the staple of much ODL, providing a permanent document that is convenient to use. Distribution may be physical or electronic. Print allows two-way communication but only with a delay. Radio has been widely used for formal and informal teaching, helping to bring teaching alive, and overcoming the problems of physical distribution that may limit print.

Television has obvious merits but tends to have costs ten times those of radio. Cassettes have been used for similar purposes to radio, overcoming the problems of timing that limit the use of broadcast radio. Videoconferencing allows specialists at a centre to reach scattered audiences provided they have the equipment to take part.

Many videoconference systems allow for one-way video and two-way audio so that, for some of the audience, it becomes a two-way medium. A variety of computer-based technologies have been used including the distribution of sample lesson plans on CD-ROMs, setting up exchanges by computer conference between teachers' colleges, encouraging the interactive use of computer-based learning materials, encouraging the use of web-based materials, and using computer conferencing to encourage discussion among learners.

In making choices the planner is likely to be influenced above all by the convenience of the learner, the cost, and the need for a culture of maintenance. It will be necessary to maintain hardware and software: physical equipment needs maintenance and access to specialist staff and supplies. Software will need updating and improving on a regular basis.

While ODL does not demand that we use the new, computer-based, technologies, they present enough opportunities to consider them separately. The development of computer links is beginning to blur the distinction drawn above between distribution and teaching. It is possible, through an internet connection, both to distribute material to learners electronically rather than physically and to teach them, by means of a computer programme, or engage in dialogue with them by email or computer conferencing. New communication technologies are being used with four different functions in teacher education.

i) The first is simply to distribute teaching materials; from the educator's point of view it may make little difference if materials are distributed by post or by the internet, though the implications in terms of cost and convenience for the user may be very different.

ii) Second, in some cases electronic communications allow simulated two-way communication. This is the case where a trainee teacher interacts with a computer programme instead of with a tutor.

iii) Third, where computers are networked, or students have access to the internet, then computer-based technologies can be used for two-way or multi-way communication.

iv) Fourth, there is increasing diversification into resource-based, self-access teacher education in a variety of media. A range of dedicated websites have been created for the professional development of teachers. Wherever teachers have access to the internet, these sites can increase the exchange of materials and interaction between teachers and direct them to other teacher education resources, experts and professional associations.

Computer-mediation of knowledge production and consumption is progressing rapidly within all levels of education. 'Knowledge for profit' is being seriously assessed, and actively pursued globally, by the managers of public and private tertiary institutions. It is increasingly possible for shareholders to buy a piece of the 'knowledge industry', in which the exigencies of profit, loss, and costs of production are the primary determinants of what is to be learned and taught.

The electronic transmission of knowledge has set off waves of competition between universities to cut labour costs and to increase the number of fee paying students. This atmosphere is part of the mega-context within which teachers and learners must collaborate. From the teacher/learner perspective, much has been made of the social and pedagogical 'effects' of the transformation of knowledge by technical means.

Pedagogically, the most positive discursive claims appear to be that hypertext undermines the center of political and ideological control, permitting a learner to "choose his or her own centre of investigation and experience"; virtual text appears on the computer screen as a digital reconstitution of reading as writing, destabilising the teacher-writer/student-reader hierarchy; the design of the technology embodies a non-linear rationality that liberates thought from the shackles of a mechanistic worldview; and finally, hypertext promotes epistemological pluralism by positing multiple interpretations of the world. Therefore, the goals of teaching and the act of teaching coincide in a socially meaningful context guided by maxims, or presuppositions, about the act of knowing, and what it is that must be known. The meaning of 'pedagogy', in content rather than form, applied to the medium of hypertext-based teaching, has yet to be critically examined with reference to economics.

Pedagogical artefacts such as computers and texts mediate the transmission of ideas. The role of education was seen as confined to the transmission of those norms and values assumed to be required by the labour market. Unveiling the hidden curriculum was the central point of their endeavour, as the superficial appearance of the curriculum was considered to be inconsequential.

Knowledge is not deterministically set by the structures of social formations, being transmitted unproblematically through pedagogical systems. Ideas are hegemonic only to the extent that they embody common sense propositions. Further, the technologies employed in teaching are not neutral applications that simply guide the learner; rather the artefacts of educational technology are themselves the products of social shaping, and are implicated in the reproduction and legitimisation of social knowledge and inequalities.

The conceptual, symbolic and physical artefacts of pedagogy provide both the means and the object of our critique, through which teachers/learners come to accept or to challenge the status and legitimacy of dominant knowledge claims. Knowledge is embedded in a "set of cultural practices which are encoded in language, resulting in the creation of a set of texts, whose emphases and omissions help to construct what a subject means and what it means to know".

In order to elicit a 'revolutionary process', computer-mediated-communication must be constructed through an active intermental collaboration of learners with teachers. The goal is to articulate a new, more fertile intra-mental understanding by both learners and teachers. Preparation of the 'online' material should permit both teacher and learner to reflect on the new material, discuss tentative understandings with others, actively search for more information to throw light on areas of interest or difficulty, and build conceptual connections.

The hypertext produces a revolution in pedagogy, rests crucially on an *a priori* progressive narrative; that is, a belief in technological progress and in the universally beneficent effects of technology 'in the long run'. This was done by viewing both the technology and the education involved as a socially collaborative process. Computer-mediated-education renders a new form of teaching/learning. The technology involved is not a first cause. It should be viewed as a collection of social artefacts created within, not outside of socio-economic circumstances.

A growing divide between nations, races, rural/urban sectors or individuals regarding access to new technologies are considered to be only problems of transition. The information 'superhighway' is offered up as a powerful moral and political imperative giving all of us the means of transit from an industrial to information economy.

Inequalities in access to pedagogical tools are not confined to 'less developed' countries. The language is constructed in accounting terms. The actions of those, in control of the resources for hypertext learning, might be described as constructing pedagogy in accordance with the principles and priorities of the market. The idea that universities must be better prepared to compete for students in a global marketplace becomes the focus of attention.

In these terms, the ideas of class, gender, equity, collaborative learning, or pedagogical epistemology, become irrelevant as focal categories. Commodification of education becomes the primary concern. Rational behaviour moves away from the pursuit of knowledge for its own sake, to "one of the main enterprises of the future post-industrial economy". The university is reconstructed as a supply side mechanism to advance the goals of economic rationalism and global reform.

From this perspective, information technology enables unprecedented centralisation of control over production of both things and knowledge, and a simultaneous dispersion of work and study around the globe. Both workplace solidarity and student communalism become anachronisms. The computer transforms value into exchange-value through the permutation of all types of knowledge into commodity forms.

Technologies that mediate human activity are bound up with the accumulation process evolving through history, and yet remain the means for active resistance to that process. Human activity provides the fabric of history, the dynamic shaping of both material and cultural worlds, the unifying process of object and subject, the creative force for change.

The information technologies which mediate human activity in the late twentieth century are neither a product of, nor embodiment of, fixed relations; neither "rotten fruit of futurist fancy" nor "ideology in the guise of social analysis". Pedagogy is not a 'tool' for transformation; it is neither a determining process nor a finished product.

When learners use computer tools in ways which pay attention to the attributes of concepts and their interrelationships, then they are employing contextual thinking and learning. When they use the same tools to create links between material in a haphazard fashion, they are gathering information which may or may not lead to knowledge. The potential of computer mediation to foster knowledge depends less on what learners use, than on how they use it.

ROLE OF ICTs

ICTs are being used by teachers and learners in conventional universities and colleges as well as in tertiary institutions, which serve the needs of distance learners who are home-based or in some other off-campus location. They can enable distance learners to receive and interact with educational material and resources, to engage with teachers and peers in ways that previously may have been impossible.

The computer offers the student an opportunity to interact physically with the learning material on a symbolic level, whereas the other media—at the physical level—only allow for browsing and repetition. This possibility for interaction on the symbolic level is what makes the computer unique. The computer is no longer one option or one choice of media among others in a media mix as it was considered a few years back, when computers primarily were used for word-processing, e-mail and computer conferencing.

The computer has other options because it relies on a new language using a binary code (0 and 1) which is able to handle both signs, visuals, sounds and other kinds of formal systems in approximately the same way as the alphabet supports print and written language. The computer is an integrated medium for:

i) production (paper, pencil, typewriter, brush, etc.)
ii) preparation (content, form, layout, etc.)
iii) storage (book, library, database, etc.)
iv) copying (printing, copy machine, etc.)
v) search (index, catalogue, etc.)
vi) distribution (mail)
vii) communication (telephone, fax)

But this development has not been supported so much by 'the computer as a machine' similar to the radio and television monitor as by 'the computer as a medium' using a digital communications system different from the analogue system used in other media.

The advantage of the computer is the use of digital information processing, but this way of handling data is about to be integrated into other media. At the moment most telephone communication is digital at least in the Western world, and television will become digital within a few years offering the users High Definition Television, a multiplication of available programmes and several interactive services. Especially, families connected to cable-television will have these new options and providers of cable-television are at the moment exploring the possibilities of offering telecommunication facilities as telephony, e-mail and internet access through the cables exchanging the remote-control with a small keyboard.

In practice it restricts the possibilities of using multimedia in home-based education to stand-alone systems like CD-ROM and excludes facilities like the WWW and e-mail—at least for the next years. As a consequence of these limitations for computer networking the educational providers may place confidence in digital interactive television.

The working distance towards the computer is 50-60 centimetres, towards the television screen the normal distance is 2-5 metres depending on the size of the screen. In front of the computer you sit in a upright position similar to the one at your desk, in front of the television you sit relaxed in an armchair. These differences has to be respected.

Educational material on the computer has to respect the equality between the learner and the learning material—the computer supports an anti-authoritarian mode of communication in learning. The CD-ROM as a medium contains both signs, visuals and sound organised in a way open for interactive processing by the user/learner. At the same time the CD-ROM also is a medium for storage of huge amount of data (information) and for distribution via sales or mail of these data.

There are three levels of communication (media) specific interplay in learning, reflecting, at the same time, the different types of educational communication—synchronous and asynchronous (stored and delayed) communication. Interaction in educational communication is also, basically, dealing with presentation of information. Although, the learner has a possibility to interact with the learning material the communication is one-way. Interactive media are stand-alone systems in which all the information is stored before the interaction begins. Interactive media are more suitable for presentation of information organised along logic-didactic lines than for presentation as narratives. Interactive media may be ranked in four categories according to levels of possible interaction:

i) browsing
ii) consultation
iii) games
iv) hypothesis testing

Interaction organised as browsing and consultation are primarily used in sender-oriented presentations of information in which the user may choose between certain routes through the material. Consultation allows for more sophisticated search options than browsing. Interactive systems organised as games or built for hypothesis testing are more user oriented allowing the user to follow his own path through the material.

Games create a closed world of its own in which the players move around following different paths according to the rules of the game. But in a perspective of learning this becomes problematic because the absorption in a game is contradictionary to reflection and contemplation which are the goals of learning.

At the moment it is not possible to integrate a communication dimension directly in interactive multimedia such as the CD-ROM and the WWW. References to educational material in these formats can only be circulated as quotations which puts rather heavy limitations on a possible (wanted) dialogue. Of course, this does not deprive the CD-ROM and other interactive multimedia of their excellent qualities when it comes to displaying data in a format where it is easily retrieval.

CD-ROM and WWW are especially important for the transference of knowledge-learning-within subject areas in which the knowledge may be organised according to logical and hierarchic principles. The hyper structure of these media supports the interaction between the learner and the learning material, while, at the same time, the learner remains in a position where he or she controls the learning process.

The relationship between past, present and future is integrated in the interplay between the time of narration and the time of the narrated. At the same time the narrative presentation creates a 'space' in which the learner may reflect together with the narrator—or guided by the narrator—upon the events and characters in the narrated story. This leaves the learner with an option for a virtual, but guided interaction with the story which from a learning perspective is comparable to the physical interaction in interactive media.

APPLICATIONS OF ICT-BASED DISTANCE LEARNING

Home-based lifelong learning systems are emerging with the help of ICTs such as radio, television receivers, video receivers, telephone lines, computer mediated communication (CMC) and the internet. The home-based learners undertake their studies are complex and highly varied, and these can impact upon the educational process and its results as well. As far as learning at home is concerned, it is important to pay attention to the social relationships within the domestic setting, and it is also necessary to take account of the nature of the relationships between learners and the technology.

Unlike students attending a university campus, home-based learners need to fit their studies into times and spaces. For they often face conflicting claims. Those in paid employment have a limited amount of time available for learning and there are competing demands upon those non-work hours, such as domestic responsibilities, leisure interests and socialising, etc. The context and circumstances of home-based learners vary from country to country and even from region to region within a country.

Home-based learners can find a place in their homes where they can study relatively undisturbed during some part of the day and/or night. However, the room in which they can study text materials quietly is often not the place in which media equipment (e.g., television, video, computer, telephone, etc.) can be accessed. Where these items tend to be located is in communal family space and there is often competition among family members for the use of equipment. Within the households, the quality of access to ICT afforded to individual members varies: patterns of use of domestic technologies reflect existing social relationships with differences in terms of gender and age, etc.

The nature of how media technologies are perceived and utilised is not uniform; it can vary from person to person and between households. For example, men and women, adults and children might envisage the main purpose of the telephone or the computer in very different ways; each will have his own conceptions of the function of various technologies and his capacity to connect with or isolate them from other people. Similarly, one household might use the video recorder or internet access in marked contrast to another. There can be enormous differences between Western countries and Eastern countries, between developed countries and developing countries.

In many Asian countries, where households typically contain an extended family and the total domestic space is generally restricted, home-based learners have to develop strategies to maximise their "undisturbed" time or "undisturbed" places for learning. So they have to lessen their social activities, study very late at night or wake up earlier to learn, undertake their studies in other locations, for example, while commuting or at the workplace during break times or after everyone else has gone home. The use of media-based learning materials can impose constraints, because students may only be able to access those materials at times and locations that are restricted. This is the case in Western countries; it has even more significance in many Asian countries.

The access to ICTs varies from country to country, from region to region. For example, early in 1995, per 1,000 inhabitants there were 805 television receivers and 626 main telephone lines in USA, 684 television receivers and 488 main telephone lines in Japan. In the UK, domestic television and telephone services have reached saturation levels by 1996, 99 per cent of households contained at least one television receiver, almost 94 per cent of those had a telephone.

In Asia, where open and distance education has increased a great deal in recent years, the access to media technologies varies enormously from country to country, from region to region, with only very few having domestic penetration rates for television and telephones that are similar to those in the Western world.

Globally, the situation of learning at home with ICTs is not so optimistic or desirable, either in the Western countries or in the Eastern ones. In mid-1998, just 28 per cent of households contained a computer and less than one-third of those have access to the internet. Canadian internet access statistics illustrate that approximately half of Athabasca University students do not have internet at home. The case of Asia is not better, its computer access follows a very similar pattern to that of television and telephones, with only a proportion of domestic PCs having a network connection.

Only the minority of students could afford the costs of this education which heavily relies on ICTs. Modern distance education is a kind of education based on advanced technologies such as multimediated computer, mobile communication facilities, digitised and wide-screen television, etc. Owning these technologies could enable advantages to be taken of such advanced education.

Common learners could not afford online education, which requires very significant costs for the learners to equip and regularly re-equip himself or herself as a lifelong learner, to fund the costs of the consumables of learning, to pay the connection charges, and to pay directly for tutorial and mentoring support and for access to databases and information. In many developing Asian countries and regions, it is obviously inappropriate to consider heavy reliance upon ICTs for home-based learning, except for particular well-defined and well-provided groups of learners; these are usually located in large urban areas.

Open and distance teaching institutions that seek to reach widely dispersed students face a dilemma: more use of ICTs will be demanded by affluent urban-dwelling students, while such innovations are likely to do little for those students and potential students who are disconnected from ICTs.

The reality for most learners is that they must find their own best way of combining the demands of studying with their other commitments. Individual context is clearly paramount; each student has to determine a pattern of study, home and work life that fits his or her circumstances and needs. Distance educators need to be aware of the environments within which home-based learning using ICTs takes place and obstacles with which students will possibly find when planning and designing the instructional programmes, courses, learning resources.

The distance instruction programmes and course design should enable individual learners the flexibility to plan and execute a personal study pattern that meets their particular needs. The use of ICTs for home-based learning, two levels of institutional planning and decision making are necessary: at one level, strategic decisions are needed; at another level, tactical decisions must be made.

Many limiting factors which mean that few home-based learners cannot take the advantages of ICTs, and there are quantitative concerns that distance educators need to address. However, two radical problems must be settled: one is to strengthen student counselling; the other is to provide convenient services, such as accommodating the access to the internet and borrowing resources for learning.

Some researchers find that a large number of learners can neither make optimum use of ICTs, nor do they know how to use them effectively. Therefore, it is necessary to develop training programmes to improve the students' learning skills as well as the capabilities of managing time. Supporting students in developing new skills associated with using the media can enhance the students' performance effectively.

WOMEN'S USE OF ICTs IN ODL COURCES

Women in the developing world are relatively well represented in education and training opportunities provided through distance and open learning. Women are not equitably represented in ODL courses in all countries, and there is significant variation both between and within regions. In Africa, men greatly outnumber women in most distance learning programmes, and this is true whether or not ICTs are the delivery medium, and appears to hold for both formal and non-formal training. Women tend to be the majority in adult literacy classes and traditional birth attendants' health programmes.

In the Asian countries most of the ODL enrolment figures cited were much closer to parity between male and female students, with the exception being those presented for India. The Sri Lanka report finds no gender disparity in women's enrolment in schools and tertiary educational institutions, and no apparent difference in trends between conventional universities and ODL institutions. Women represent 60 per cent of the students following external degree programmes.

In India, the enrolment of women in Indira Gandhi National Open University (IGNOU) was 28.4 per cent in 1998. The University of the South Pacific is the largest provider of ODL courses in the region with a total of 4,204 enrolments in 2000, and 48 per cent were women.

Many of the barriers women face in accessing ODL using ICTs are the same ones they face when accessing education of any kind. Illiteracy was raised as the major barrier to women's education for most African and Asian countries. In most sub-Saharan African countries, about 70 per cent of adult women are illiterate with similar figures for those Asian countries that cited data.

The challenge of illiteracy must be overcome before women can benefit from ICTs. In the South Pacific the issue of illiteracy was mainly raised for women in the rural areas and outer islands. In the Caribbean, female illiteracy was not viewed as a gender-based barrier.

Poverty and lack of economic power is borne much more by women than men. As a result, women have much less access to disposable income for expenditures related to education. Women are generally not engaged in their own economic activities and very few women have money. All the regions made reference to the fact that women have less time to learn because of heavy domestic chores.

In Kenya, a programme called Regional Reach provides rural populations with information in local languages through community screening of video-tapes focusing on current social problems. And, in a majority of households, most career women still bear the brunt of household chores. The broader socio-cultural factors that perpetuate women's inequality in society, and hence undervalue their need for education, were raised mainly by the African and Asian countries.

The importance of the role women teachers can play in balancing gender disparities is acknowledged in government education policies in some regions. The absence of female role models can particularly reinforce gender stereotyping in the fields of science, mathematics and technology. Even in the Caribbean countries, where there is a higher proportion of women than men in tertiary education, a concern was raised about the tendency for women to restrict themselves to socially accepted, non-technological streams.

The impact of all the factors—illiteracy, poverty, time famine and socio-cultural restrictions—can severely restrict a woman's mobility. This lack of mobility can hamper a woman's ability to benefit from educational opportunities if she needs to travel some distance to access the courses, or if the courses are offered at a time or place that is either unsafe or culturally prohibited. One of the most significant barriers to women's access to education (with or without ICTs) is the lack of relevancy of the content.

When learning strategies fail to value women's knowledge, wisdom and experience, the education is not perceived as valuable to them. Since this is such a pivotal barrier in the potential for women to access educational opportunities. The barriers can be summed up in three major categories:

i) relevancy,
ii) availability and
iii) usage.

Relevancy is the most significant barrier affecting women's access to ODL delivered by ICTs. Unless the content delivered by ICTs has a direct impact on women's lives, they will not have an incentive to tackle any barriers. As for availability, although most barriers to the availability of technology apply equally to men and women, many are particularly acute in remote and rural areas. As a result, the impact on women is more severe, since more women than men usually reside in such regions. Usage includes barriers such as high costs, lack of skills and information, and socio-cultural barriers that restrict women's usage of ICTs for ODL.

The major barrier to the use of ICTs for women is its lack of relevancy to their lives. Before women even attempt to address the access barriers posed by the use of ICTs, they need a very good reason to do so. Women encounter barriers to the use of ICTs when the learning content is not directly relevant to their livelihood, and when it does not value their knowledge, wisdom and experience. If the instructional design and learning strategies are not gender-appropriate, women fail to reap the potential benefits of ODL.

The lack of technology is a significant barrier to the use of ICTs for ODL, both for the more traditional ICTs such as audio and video, and radio and television broadcasting, as well as for the newer computer-based ICTs. Universal access to more traditional forms of ODL equipment, including radios, televisions, audio and videocassette players is a problem in most countries, especially in rural regions. Whatever limited access there may be to computers and the Internet is usually concentrated in the urban centres, and most often found at the workplace rather than in people's homes.

In Africa radio is often cited as the medium most accessible to rural women. A needs analysis of two poorer districts in Kenya found relatively high percentages of women listen to the radio and only 33 per cent had a cassette player. In Bangladesh, the Bangladesh Open University has to limit its use of radio, television and audio/videocassettes because of lack of appropriate equipment at the grassroots level and lack of infrastructure needed for widespread dissemination. In Sri Lanka, an attempt was made to solve the lack of equipment through the use of study centres, but even access to the equipment in the study centres remained a problem for women because of a combination of factors—difficulty reaching the centre, lack of time and socio-cultural barriers.

Lack of access to a communications infrastructure that allows for the use of the new ICTs in ODL is a problem, at some level, for all countries. The issue was most often emphasised by the African countries—with the problem being most severe in rural areas. In Kenya, there are serious problems with internet connections or "dial-up" using a telephone line because the bandwidth is low, the line signal is of poor quality, congestion causes "traffic jams", and line breakdowns happen due to either natural or physical calamities. As well, satellite breakdowns may cut off all forms of telecommunications between Kenya and the outside world.

Problems with access to electricity are most extreme for the African countries. In many African countries electricity is available only in towns and in a very few rural areas. Only 8 per cent of Kenyan homes have power, largely in the urban areas, and only 10 per cent of the population in Tanzania has access to electricity. In Zimbabwe rural areas are not wired electronically. Only clinics, hospitals, shops and about half of the secondary schools are linked to the electric grid.

Lack of internet access poses a problem for most of the countries. Access to computer equipment is short-lived without access to technical support and, in most countries, this is at a premium. There is a lack of access to technical information, computer parts and repair services. High rates of technological obsolescence are another problem. The costs may be prohibitive, the learner may not have the necessary skills, the learner may not be aware of the service and/or the socio-cultural conditions may inhibit the learner's access.

Although there is interplay between costs and all the other barriers, costs can pose such a significant barrier, they need to be highlighted on their own. Either acquiring or accessing the necessary equipment required to use ICTs for ODL may have significant cost components. If learners needs to incur the capital cost of purchasing the equipment, they also face the high costs of maintenance and of obsolescence. In addition, the costs of powering the technology, whether by electricity or battery, can be prohibitive. With the use of newer ICTs, access to the internet through an Internet Service Provider (ISP) may be another learner expense and internet connection can be expensive.

High telephone charges may inhibit users from either using the telephone for more traditional tutor support or to go online. Telephone installation costs slightly more than $100 and the monthly payment depends on usage. Course fees are another cost that may be incurred by learners in order to access ODL courses. If a course is more expensive to produce and deliver because of the use of ICTs, those additional costs may be passed on to the learners.

The use of any technology for ODL may require the learner to acquire skills. All regions emphasised the severe barrier for women in accessing the new ICTs for ODL because of lack of computer skills. A Bangladesh survey of women professionals found that 60 per cent had no exposure at all to computers, and the computer knowledge of the remaining 40 per cent was limited to word processing. Eighty per cent of the women students of the University of the South Pacific (USP) indicated a lack of computer literacy and appropriate training to be a barrier to their use of ICTs for ODL. Along with computer literacy many ODL applications using the newer ICTs require skills in the English language.

For a rural person who may only know how to read and write in his or her local language, this feature is a major barrier. Another barrier to the use of the newer ICTs is the new learning skills they may require. Learners may need to be more self-directed in their learning and/or rely on new forms of group interaction. The lack of these skills may also be a barrier to effective usage.

The potential students are often unable to afford newspapers that might carry advertisements for ODL programmes. Women also need to know where they might access ICT equipment and training in order to participate in ODL offered by ICTs. They also need information about the broader issues around the importance of ICTs—its potential relevancy and capacity.

In Sri Lanka, ICTs are male-dominated and women are not the first to gain access and use ICTs because of cultural and socio-economic factors. In most homes, particularly in rural areas, men own the radio and television sets, sometimes making the equipment inaccessible to women even within their own home. Also in Pakistan, if computers are located in study centres, women will encounter the problem of female segregation. This problem can take a different form in urban workplaces.

ICTs can be a threat to traditional systems. In some villages, television is not allowed for cultural reasons and therefore a course on video-tape would not be very practical. The lack of confidence is reinforced by the absence of women as teachers and trainers in technical fields generally, and in ICTs training specifically. However, age was seen as a barrier to the use of ICTs for some women and rural women, mainly the poor and unemployed, are being left behind.

Before ICTs can be adopted by the ODL learner they need to be embraced by the provider. There are significant barriers that a provider encounters when moving to the use of ICTs to produce and deliver ODL. In some countries the use of ICTs have been discontinued due to high costs. The Kenya Institute for Education's radio broadcasts for schools were discontinued because charges for airtime were exorbitant. Since there is currently minimal infrastructure in many institutions offering ODL, the cost of purchasing computers would be a very large barrier.

Maintenance is a major ongoing expense for the ODL provider and one often overlooked. Lack of teacher readiness can be another significant barrier to an institution's use of ICTs for ODL. Research into barriers to the use of ICTs faced by women students of the University of the South Pacific found that academic staff lacked ICT skills. The staff also need training in adapting ODL learning material to the new electronic media and in their new roles of teacher, facilitator and mentor.

Some countries proposed specific methods to improve the relevancy of ICTs to the lives of women in order to reduce barriers to ODL. The strategies focused on three themes: work through women's organisations, work with women leaders and change agents, and develop ODL content that matters to women's lives. Strategies for ensuring content relevancy of ICTs for ODL focus on valuing women's knowledge, wisdom and experience.

Learning strategies and instructional design should be gender-appropriate and build on traditional communications methods. Participatory methods should be used to design and develop the content and learning systems to reflect the lives of women. ICTs should be designed and used appropriately so as to overcome literacy barriers, and the use of local language content should be considered.

Women in rural communities, in particular, need to be able to access the kind of training most relevant to their livelihood and also they need to be involved in software development including that which might best relate to indigenous and traditional knowledge. In Uganda, online organisations for women to operate as information hubs by distributing information from the internet to the community. Groups and organisations for women should be encouraged to develop their own internet-related projects.

The most effective way to ensure access by women to ICTs for ODL is to use appropriate technology. ODL should be learner-centred, and the medium should be selected based on an assessment of the learner needs, taking into account the desired knowledge and skills, as well as the broader technical environment. Many effective strategies use a multimedia, multifaceted approach, sometimes combining the traditional with the modern.

In the University of the South Pacific, ODL activities proposed a blended approach to the issue of appropriate technology. For people in rural areas in the South Pacific, print packages are still the best mode for learning, and radio also provides a viable alternative. In the future, telecentres may provide isolated populations with access to ICTs. Women preferred a mixed mode of learning which would include face-to-face and online delivery and communication.

In many countries literacy barriers mean that technology cannot be "appropriate" if it relies on the written word. Certainly, in many regions of many countries, any technology that required literacy in the English language would not be "appropriate technology". For all these reasons, using appropriate technology would rule out the use of computer-based ICTs for ODL for many countries and regions.

However, while acknowledging this reality, none of the regions wanted to cut off any part of their population from the potential benefits of the digital revolution in the long term. There was unanimous support for pursuing policies and programmes to develop ICTs to widen access to quality educational opportunities. As well, there was general recognition of the potential for ICTs, even now, to meet the needs of some groups of women. It was emphasised that providing education using the new technologies will not only help students learn but also equip them with ICT skills.

The concept of telecentres to provide access to ICTs was almost universally endorsed. In some cases the centres were seen as an extension of the ODL institution. Other ICTs such as television and radio may be better alternatives at least for now. In experience with telecentres from both Sri Lanka and the South Pacific provides support for examining carefully the telecentre solution.

In Sri Lanka an attempt was made to solve the problem of lack of equipment through the use of regional study centres equipped with audiocassettes, videocassettes and computers. Surveys of a teacher education programme found that utilisation of the technology provided at the centres was poor for the following reasons: non-availability of transport facilities, the nature of terrain which made even walking difficult, and cultural inhibitions and household chores not permitting long hours away from home.

In the South Pacific, USP provided equipment access through study centres and research found that access was still a major barrier for female students. The small number of computers was aggravated by staff use of the computers for their own work, the centres' restricted hours and a lack of maintenance skills. As well, costs of transport to the centres were prohibitive.

There was universal support for providing training to women and girls so that they could access ICTs for ODL. A major emphasis was placed on the need for women to take on the role of trainer/educator. By training women to train others, they pass along skills and, at the same time, serve as role models. Women should be trained in such a way that they can build on their skills, and on-the-job training should be encouraged. They should be trained not just as users of ICTs for ODL. They should be trained in both hardware and software skills, as content developers, and as providers of user support and technical support.

Once women are engaged as learners using ICTs for ODL, the need for support is critical. Research done at Indira Gandhi National Open University (IGNOU) found that many problems experienced by ODL students are common to both genders, but they become more acute in the case of women. The most severe problems were irregular and unsystematic tutorial help, inadequate supply of reading material and lack of study centres. Some countries are working on development policies, including those on education and telecommunications, which are designed to raise gender awareness. Some other countries, saw the need for education and telecommunications policy makers to collaborate to support women's use of ICTs.

NETWORKED ODL: CHALLENGES AHEAD

Over the past years, networks of different nature have been established between traditional universities and their partners that facilitate networked e-learning or ODL, especially in higher education. A broad spectrum of these networks already exists for a long time and new ones are daily popping up, on a more local scale, either on an international level.

There are four types of networks:

i) *Discipline-based networks* refer to networking of individuals or groups (departments) with a common research interest. These (thematic) networks have mainly been developed for the improvement of (joint) research activities, but they also spark educational initiatives. Their strength lies primarily in a firm base of contents-related expertise.

ii) *Profession-based networks* refer to networking of organisational units in universities in charge of education and training for a particular professional profile (e.g., engineering or medicine). The value of such a network is mainly based on the internationalisation of education, bringing together teachers and students across borders, giving them a flavour of the world where they will exercise their profession.

iii) *Institution-based networks* refer to networking at the level of the university management. The aim of these networks is strategic cooperation based on the potential of synergy for policy development and the possibility of economic benefits.

iv) *Service-based networks* refer to networking of central services at universities that offer central support for the implementation of ICTs in education. The strength of these networks lies in the possibility of pooling resources and services and of exchanging expertise.

The implementation of ODL in a networked environment offers a great potential, like flexibility, joint course development, or cost sharing. But, in spite of the various efforts that have been invested in the different e-learning networks, there is still a great reluctance to embark on large-scale activities that are self-sustainable and permanently embedded in mainstream education.

When trying to introduce ODL successfully within a single institute, one is often confronted with a number of problems that need to be solved. Doing the same in a networked environment opens great opportunities, but introduces at the same time new obstacles that are specific to the network context. An online setting provides a level of flexibility and convenience not provided by traditional classroom courses. Learning via the web means flexibility in the delivery of learning content and courses, and also a quick and easy updating of the content. Learning opportunities are provided in a more flexible and customer-aware manner: choices and options concerning content and learning mode become wider and more easily tailored to suit individual learning styles and circumstances.

ODL increases a broader participation in learning: not only is there flexibility towards the traditional audience and the new target groups, it is also possible to 'accommodate' more students and to expand the student population. The opportunity to widen the range of potential students through online learning can help make programmes struggling with small enrolments locally sustainable. The learning environment becomes accessible to all.

It can be meaningful for people of all ages, it can reach new, non-traditional and/or remote audiences that cannot attend classes on campus, lifelong learners and international students, and can also reach disadvantaged regions and individuals. The increasing access to high level learning opportunities to people who would not otherwise benefit from them for physical, economic or organisational reasons benefits the democratisation of the learning experience. Only inter-university networking will allow the creation of a full e-learning offer to remote audiences.

International networking can provide a European dimension, sharing international learning experience in education and training by cross-border delivery of courses, by using collaborative learning of students of different countries. Students come in contact and can work collaboratively with students from other countries and cultures. It gives educators, trainers and learners with different worldviews the opportunity to exchange ideas and information, and learn from each other, thus expanding each participant's global view and gaining a broader perspective on a specific subject as well as on the world in general.

Institutions enter an international and competitive marketplace. They perceive that ICT will enable them to increase their market share and to extend its influence in an academic area. There is also the need for the university to be seen "keeping up with the competition". It gives extra-institutional visibility to excellent knowledge and knowhow developed in a given university. The university can decide to capitalise on the institution's existing "brand" name, in a quest for increasing profit. Transnational cooperation between universities is needed to disseminate scientific knowledge in targeted education and training settings.

Where pedagogy of ICT-based education and training is still largely missing, well-balanced joint research can lead to faster and better results. Networking can help the ODL institutions in overcoming the problem of professional marketing and sales of their educational and training services, which is precondition of reaching the "critical number" of learners, sufficient to cover the cost of development and delivery of quality courses.

Functions such as the development and distribution of learning materials, tuition, assessment, online registration and record-keeping, award-granting, learner support, and general administration can now be shared through a wide variety of organisational arrangements marked by specialisation and "added-value" partnerships involving both the public and private sectors. Universities and teachers can only create the necessary high quality learning materials and services by joining their efforts and resources.

From an institution's and teacher's point of view the use and sharing of international resources is a considerable advantage and result in economies of scale. The creation of a database for reusable learning and teaching materials will get a far greater number of entries, and its maintenance may become more cost-effective by sharing costs and income. It helps capitalisation of 'teaching acts' as reusable learning resources.

Networking gives opportunities to universities to collaborate not only on the design and development of courses but also on the delivery of courses, and on internet or web based education materials and curricula. New degrees of collaborative work between geographically disparate teams are possible. Networked learning provides a large number of learners with quick access not only to the course instructors.

Interuniversity networking will allow the creation of a full e-learning offer to distance learners, e.g., home learners and part-time learners. The student gets automatically access to a more global virtual campus in which lectures, seminars, etc., given at any of the partner universities are made accessible to everyone through the network (virtual classes). Infrastructure and resources of each university are made available at the other campuses.

Students are thus provided with a more attractive offer, by extending the own programme and courses that are only available in partner universities. This encourages the learners' autonomy and gives them a broader choice on what, how and when to learn.

Online learning can be at least as cost-effective as face-to-face teaching. Moreover, the development of virtual delivery models will most likely result in a higher degree of cost-effectiveness and a cost reduction. Costs can be reduced through standardisation, resource sharing, economies of scale, increased productivity, by purchasing hard- and software jointly. Travel costs can be lowered. There is a potential to share costs and to distribute risk.

For the critical mass, highly specialised courses both at the level of availability of expertise for development and at the level of availability of participating students to create a cost-effective production, can be offered. Productivity can be increased and expansion enabled without cost increases. Funding can be attracted more easily where several universities come together and resources pooled for maximum impact.

Distance education programmes can also be not only self-supporting but can generate additional funds to support other departments at a traditional institution. Through networking the institutions might enhance the quality of their programmes, add a European dimension to their offerings and establish attractive virtual and physical mobility schemes for their students. It helps teachers to reconsider their routine practice and to add innovative and quality elements in their courses to match the requests of a transnational collaboration and of increased usability of teaching activity.

Networking can also contribute to the quality of education by organised introduction and operation of quality assurance systems and offering comprehensive approach to accreditation and benchmarking. There is a belief that environments that include technology can improve efficiency and/or effectiveness of student learning.

On the pedagogical/practical level one should be aware of cultural, social, and/or political differences among a group of learners, educators and trainers, when making a distance-learning course for an international audience. The types of distance learning available, the technologies required of students and educators/trainers, and the way course content is structured and presented all need to be planned with a multicultural, multinational audience in mind. Subjects, or approaches to it, may be taboo in some cultures or countries.

Cultural differences may also affect the way in which people (man/women) work in group or individually. Cultural barriers, especially those influencing learning styles should be tackled. In different countries there may be a different approach towards learning and its appreciation. Obstacles to change are closely associated with the established practices and cultural traditions of the teaching faculty.

Online materials must be subjected to the rigours of quality assurance. Quality assurance systems should be put in place to ensure quality of curriculum, environment, teaching and learning, assessment and student support. Quality standards must be developed to ensure quality in all university programmes.

In order for distance delivered courses to maintain a level of credibility within the institution and outside of it, it is important that the same faculty governance processes that are used to approve the face-to-face courses be used to approve distance-delivered courses. Lack of support for the teachers on a pedagogical level remains an obstacle.

Designing and developing a course to be effectively delivered at a distance requires the use of an instructional designer or another professional who understands the medium of delivery as well as adult learning theory and learning styles. Instructors have negative perceptions of technology-supported learning and ODL. They prefer a face-to-face learning environment and cannot see the educational benefits or are ignorant on the potential of new ICT-based methods.

The web and the internet are indeed technologies that require a fundamental rethinking of teaching practice. Teaching and learning in a network of universities means that people involved are located at different places accessing the network from behind their computer screen. It is often feared that interpersonal contact and attention are lacking.

On the level of the institution itself, the universities also fear to lose control and autonomy and the power that was historically in the hands of the institution. When cooperating with other universities the challenge is to turn the traditional loose structures from joint project management or thematic networks into sustainable committed collaborations among universities with common academic interests.

Technology-based learning also poses a new challenge to the students who become more and more a 'teacher' themselves, and become independent, self-directed learners, and constructors of knowledge. On the organisational level distance or distributed education requires a great deal of coordination and in many instances, a redefinition of the faculty role.

Teachers and faculty often are reticent to embrace the use of ICT caused by a lack of teaching skills for successful teaching at a distance. Staff will need an adequate training in the running of distance courses, and not one limited to how to use computers or software. The institution should provide teachers and staff with help and training in the use of learning technologies, organisation of ODL learning and production of learning materials that support self-centred learning.

In a distributed environment it is a challenge for the university to provide textbooks, materials (especially non-electronic learning materials), but also things such as T-shirts, university trinkets, software and supplies to the student population. Coordination and planning problems may emerge because of learners and teachers working in different time zones.

Institutions offering programmes across countries should take care of some administrative problems. Traditional enrolment may be inappropriate for distance learners. Universities may want and need to rethink enrolment periods and investigate how their internal systems can support enrolments or registrations via telephone, voice-mail, fax, the internet and how to obtain "real" signatures from students.

Interactive multimedia courseware development is a labour intensive project and requires synergy among faculty experts, programmers, and digital artists. When instructors in traditional institutions are asked to participate in distance education programmes this is often in addition to their normal course loads.

Motivation is important on both a pedagogical, technological and organisational level. Introduction of information and communication technologies in education requires that students as well as instructors themselves are interested and motivated to learn how to work with computers, to learn how technology can be used efficiently in education. On the other hand, it is inappropriate that every university develops its own delivery platforms. Systems and platforms should be compatible, materials interchangeable. Content and technical standards need to be adopted that will optimise interoperability with other institutions in areas such as the creation of learning objects databases, information databases, libraries, administrative systems and learner support strategies as well as the facilitation of interactions among learners and teachers.

Building such an educational repository that provides access to learning objects requires standards and structures that can facilitate object storage, retrieval and aggregation to suit the needs of learners or the pedagogical intentions of instructional developers. Security deficiencies have to be solved and the network should be protected against viruses. On the attitudinal level students can be frustrated by the computer and network facilities available to them or by features in the electronic tools they are being asked to use.

On the practical level, virtual education is often limited by the lack of appropriate technical infrastructure. Lack of technical background, lack of basic computer literacy of the students as well as of the instructors and at the support side, are an obstacle in introducing ICTs in education. Due to these lack of technical skills it should be prevented that ICTs are used at a level below potential.

Networked and computer-based learning cause an increase in costs for the organisation: costs to develop and deliver online courses, the cost for the technical infrastructure. Especially the front-end costs associated with the development of ICT infrastructure and ICT-based instructional materials are difficult for organisations to finance without a substantial reallocation of current resources.

The distance education student buys the cheapest educational product instead of the best product. There is thus a need for substantial start-up funds to cover for the costs. On the income side distant and online courses must be priced at a sensible level. Copyright restrictions on the use of instructional products and materials in fact do not promote sharing through collaborative inter-institutional arrangements or through broad international delivery models, just like it is difficult making readings available electronically because of copyright limitations.

Copyrights can also be an obstacle while adapting courseware for meeting local needs. To receive formal agreements from the copyright owner is a time-consuming and costly exercise. Universities face a significant and growing competition from other and new types of e-learning providers. In the higher education market traditional universities not only have to compete more and more with other universities but also with virtual and commercial organisations and companies, all offering the same type of courses.

REFERENCES

Bang J., H.P. Baumeister and K.Wilson, "Collaboration as a Challenge, New Learning Environments embedded in old Traditions", in *Proceedings from EUNIS'99, Information Technology Shaping European Universities*, Helsinki, 1999.

Barron, A., K. S. Ivers and L. Sherry, "Exploring the Internet", *The Computing Teacher*, 22(2), 14-19, 1994.

Dock, A. and J. Helwig (eds.), "Interactive Radio Instruction: Impact, Sustainability and Future Directions", *Educational Training Technology Notes,* Series 4, Washington D.C., USAID/World Bank, 1999.

Euler M., and D. Von Berg, *The Use of Electronic Media in Open Learning and Distance Education*, Paris: UNESCO, 1998.

Ellsworth, J.H., *Education on the Internet*, Indianapolis: Sams Publishing, 1994.

Floor P. (ed.), *Beyond Humanities, Long-term Strategy for ODL in University Environments and Virtual Mobility*, Brussels, Coimbra Group, 1998.

Garrison, D.R., "An analysis and evaluation of audio teleconferencing to facilitate education at a distance", *The American Journal of Distance Education*, 4(3), 16-23, 1990.

Jonassen, D.H., "Applications and limitations of hypertext technology for distance learning", Paper presented at the Distance Learning Workshop, Armstrong Laboratory, San Antonio, TX, 1992.

Kell, D., et al., "Educational technology and the restructuring movement: Lessons from research on computers in classrooms", Paper presented at the Annual Meeting of the American Educational Research Association, Boston, 1990.

Miller, G., "Distance education encounters new technologies", *American Independent Study Newsletter*, Fall, 1993.

Owston, R.D., "The World Wide Web, A Technology to Enhance Teaching and Learning?", *In Educational Researcher*, 26, 1997.

Pea, R.A., "Seeing what we build together: Distributed multimedia learning environments for transformative communications", *Journal of the Learning Sciences*, 3(3), 285-299, 1994.

UNESCO, *The Experience of Internet Usage in Education, an Analytical Survey*, UNESCO Institute for Information Technologies in Education (IITE), Moscow: UNESCO/IITE, 2000.

__________, *The New Information and Comunication Technologies For the Development of Education, Science and Culture*, 161 EX/INF. 12, Paris: UNESCO, 2001.

3

Curriculum Development and Open Access

The World Conference on Education for All which took place at Jomtien, Thailand, adopted a Declaration on Education for All, that all persons should "benefit from educational opportunities to meet their basic learning needs." However, the idea of 'education for all' is still far from reality. There are millions of people around the world who failed to get these so-called "basic learning needs". For the most part, these educationally disadvantaged people live in the developing world, where they are often left behind because of gender inequality, socio-economic circumstances, physical handicaps, or the isolation of rural villages.

Open and distance learning (ODL) provides one way to help meet their basic learning needs by increasing access to educational opportunities and thereby moving towards "education for all". ODL means different things to different people, but generally it concerns using alternative and usually less resource-based approaches which characterise distance education methods and open learning, to deliver basic education and training. In fulfilling the most basic learning needs, ODL provides opportunities for vast segments of a country's population to attain literacy, numeracy, and other necessary skills.

The issue of curriculum development in ODL is one of the key areas of interest. The debate over 'core curricula' is perhaps one of the longest running in the history of education. Yet very little progress has been achieved in this area of vital concern. Unfortunately, most literacy providers have assumed that learners learn the same way within the traditionally fixed timeframe, and that instruction must follow the traditional teacher-centred format with learners congregating at a specific time in a specific location.

In most cases, curriculum has remained a list of topics to be covered with little attention to conceptualisation and learning strategies. In some cases, traditionally designed curriculum lends itself to a linear sequence of neatly packed lessons with little flexibility and opportunity left for redesign and innovations. Arguments against traditional curriculum design and development are gathering momentum in many different ways.

ODL curriculum system needs more and better focus in the new learning-teaching environment, various perspectives on curriculum and its important component-course design. The course design should move from the teacher-centred to other or learner-centred alternatives, an approach derived from a constructivist theory of learning which determines similar objectives for the curriculum. This approach is worth considering because it may, in some way, help design curriculum that is learner-centred.

One of the characteristics of the current educational paradigm is to view curriculum as "the stuff" that is delivered to learners. The emerging paradigm raises questions about the efficacy of traditional curriculum and stresses on the rights of learners to have a voice in curriculum decision-making. However, new technologies have only enriched the teaching environment, they have done little to alter the basic assumptions on what the institution and curriculum are based, suggesting that technology, in itself, does not necessarily have an impact on the curriculum, nor does technology itself lead to a learner-centred curriculum.

Learner-centred approach to curriculum designing is not a peripheral, but a crucial component of ODL programming. Such an approach places great values on the relevance, functionality and quality of programme objectives and content of learning. One of the most critical operational aspects in any literacy programme is to determine the objectives and content of learning, and to ensure their relevance and functionality as well as their quality.

Such a learner-centred approach was recently highlighted by the World Conference on Education for All. The content of ODL courses can vary widely between places, situations and objectives, and caution must be exercised while determining the content of such course(s). The curriculum developers may use the following checklist to assess and augment the relevance of objectives and content in their respective literacy programmes:

i) *Locational relevance*: urban, rural, mountainous, desert area—characteristics of the locale: local environmental condition;

ii) *Occupational relevance*: agricultural, industrial, supplementary income generation, etc.;

iii) *Gender relevance*: for men or for women, or for both;

iv) *Familial relevance*: related to child care, family learning, children's education, population planning, family income;

v) *Cultural relevance*: national and social events, local celebrations, religious practices, community characteristics, political set up;

vi) *Temporal relevance*: learning for immediate application or for long-term or future use, contemporary development and current news;

vii) *Universal relevance*: common needs for all human beings such as health.

viii) *Technological relevance*: new technological devices and their increasing use and application in daily life.

New research should focus on both the role of the content and the importance of process in the curriculum system. Traditional assumptions about curriculum need to be changed. We need to explore curriculum issues that derive from a changing focus on the purposes of literacy education. In fact, literacy curriculum means more than the literacy programme of studies.

The curriculum for literacy should contain provisions that allow acquisition of skills and construction of knowledge through a variety of interactions between the learners, the learner and the teacher, and the learner and resources in the new communication environment. Curriculum design should move from the teacher-centred to other alternatives such as the one that is guided by a learner-centred approach.

New opportunities for using technology in learning should be explored and applied with a view to designing and developing curriculum based on such a learner-centred approach. New technologies can serve as a tool that may facilitate broad curricular change. New curriculum initiatives should, for example, explore the ways in which learning occurs when learners make connections between their own experiences and the new information they are required to have in the learning process.

Fortunately, with the help of new educational technologies a high degree of learner-centred flexibility can be introduced in the curriculum, responding to today's literacy needs and contexts. Furthermore, the introduction of a large variety of productive and income-generating and, among others, relevant vocational skills such as weaving, carpentry, handicrafts, vegetable gardening, mushroom growing, poultry raising, co-operative marketing, canning, etc., should continue to be in the curriculum in most countries for different groups.

Curriculum standards that describe what teachers are supposed to teach and learners are expected to learn should, therefore, be designed in order to "provide clear, specific descriptions of the skills and that should be taught to students".

Accordingly, international literacy curriculum standards should be finalised to provide clear, specific descriptions of the skills that should be taught to the illiterate learners in developing countries. However, curriculum standards set at such a level should be flexible enough to incorporate typical national or regional characteristics, conditions and situations in developing countries.

DESIGNING OPEN SCHOOL CURRICULUM

Open schooling reaches out to underprivileged sectors of the population and provides a second chance for young and old alike to acquire the basic skills so necessary for an economically viable and socially satisfying life. Open schooling not only has different meanings but is implemented in different ways, depending on the country in which it is located and the reasons for its establishment. In 1914, the first open school programme began in Australia. The success of the school programme led to the spread of open schools to several other Australian states and territories. Open schools were then introduced in Canada in 1919 and in New Zealand in 1922.

In the 1960s, distance education expanded massively across many countries, especially in higher education as open universities. Meanwhile distance education at the primary and secondary levels in open schools was confined to only a few countries. As a result, the contemporary view of distance education is primarily associated with the open university. The open school movement, however, is an idea whose time has come. Many countries have now set up open schools for primary and secondary students, for example, in Bangladesh, India, Indonesia, South Korea, and Zambia. Initiatives to establish similar institutions are under consideration in South Africa, Egypt, China, Nigeria, and many other countries. Although having begun much later than open universities, open schools are rapidly gaining ground and some of them have quite high enrolments.

Open learning almost invariably uses distance education methods. Open learning as a paradigm refers to an educational system that allows students to choose from a wide range of courses that may be self-paced and provides a choice of educational media. Open learning emphasises entry qualities and competencies rather than the qualifications that conventional schools emphasise. In short, open learning promotes freedom to learn.

Distance education methods were first introduced to complement conventional education; that is, radio and television complemented learning in conventional schools in such countries as Nicaragua, China, Japan, and Korea. In India, educational radio in the late 1940s and television in the early 1960s were used to support conventional education. Eventually an understanding developed of the learning materials and methods most suited to distance education, and distance education methods became sophisticated enough to stand alone. That was an important step towards the emergence of open schools, since the open learning system depends on distance education methods.

Open learning is an international movement that is spreading fast. The international concern to provide education to all has given a significant impetus to open schools. The Jomtien Conference - a landmark in education - was the first significant articulation of concerns for basic education.

The emergence of open learning is directly linked to the issue of access to education. Open universities were initiated to cope with demands for places in institutions of higher learning. The issue is somewhat different for open schools. Unlike university education, school instruction is considered to be a basic right. School instruction is seen as a necessary requirement for improving the quality of life since it is relates directly to population growth, health practices, and economic activity and productivity.

Thus open schools emerged from concern about how to provide a minimum level of education to all. The situation varied from one country to another, but four distinctive features are common:

i) reaching out with education to the disadvantaged population groups in dispersed locations where conventional schools are not viable;
ii) providing a choice to students for what they want to learn;
iii) providing a safety net to school dropouts so they do not lapse into illiteracy; and
iv) providing education to those who cannot attend conventional schools for a variety of social and economic reasons, as well as to those who missed out and are now "over age".

In developing countries, open schools act as a complementary system to provide education to all, which is different from considering open schools as an alternative. The distance education used in open schools is a pedagogical alternative, but the open schools are not an alternative—they should be considered complementary education to marginalised groups in developing countries.

The design and development of programmes for open schools is an arduous process. It requires a team of professionals that may include subject specialists, educational technologists, media communication experts, graphic designers, book designers, and producers. Open schools offer courses to a pre-degree level, ranging from early childhood education to primary, secondary, and senior secondary education.

The secondary and senior secondary programmes are comparatively more popular in developing countries. Some of the new and innovative ventures include technical and vocational education courses. Open schools offer a wide range of courses that compare to the courses offered in conventional schools, which, therefore, have remained the reference point.

Since the major concern is providing education to all, mobility from open schools to conventional schools and the reverse has been a significant consideration. Open and conventional schools can be compared in three ways. One comparison emphasises commonality and comparability so that students have a better possibility of migration to conventional schools.

The students are free to choose any subject; however, they are advised to choose combinations comparable to the conventional school system if they plan to return to a conventional school or go on to college. The National Open School of India has adopted the eclectic approach. It currently offers as many as 18 courses at the senior secondary level and this is being extended to more than 40 courses, including some vocational courses. As well, technical and vocational courses are combined with academic courses for school certification at secondary and senior secondary stages. This approach has become viable largely because open schools do not have age restrictions and a significant proportion of open school students are "over-age" and will not return to college or university.

Nevertheless, school instruction being one of the major concerns of education, open schools must permit migration between open and conventional schools. Since the programmes are at various levels and bring in students with a wide range of learning skills, the instructional processes in open schools have certain distinctive features that need serious consideration. The following considerations influence the pedagogy of open schools:

i) open school students vary widely in age—from school age children to senior citizens who differ in their experience and life skills;
ii) open school students differ widely in their learning skills and, in particular, in their reading skills;
iii) open school students may not be able to afford the same amount of time to study as can a full-time student;
iv) open school students are independent learners; and
v) open schools often depend on multimedia instruction.

With these considerations in mind, open school instruction comprises a few common elements:

i) self-study print materials,
ii) electronic media,
iii) face-to-face contact sessions,
iv) student counselling, and
v) some form of student response.

Open learning depends largely on self-study print materials. Self-study print materials are usually prepared in modular formats so that flexibility can be maintained. Each module is a self-contained learning unit. Compared to a textbook, the basic feature of self-study print material is the carefully structured presentation designed to make learning easy and effective. Usually self-study print materials comprise an introduction, a statement of learning goals and objectives, and the presentation of the information in small sections, with intermediate checks to monitor learning.

The second component of open school instruction is the use of electronic media. Electronic media have long been used to augment conventional education. In open learning, this use is integral. The level of technology intervention, however, varies widely. Most common are radio and television, as not only do radio and television have a greater outreach, but they may also be cheaper than other technology.

Many countries, including China, India, Pakistan, and Indonesia, have successfully used radio and television for education. The one-way communication of radio and television is being increasingly supplemented and, in some cases, replaced by the more effective interactive technologies like audio- and video-conferencing, teleconferencing, interactive television, computer-managed learning, and intelligent tutoring systems.

The level at which technology is used is guided by the rate of technological advancement within the country, as well as by other considerations, including the number of students and their spread over a geographical area. For example, in Australia, distance education was first used in the State of Victoria in 1908. It had its beginnings in correspondence classes for young teachers in rural schools who were unable to receive personal tuition while studying for higher qualifications. The growth of distance education continued at both the primary and secondary levels and spread to all other Australian states and territories.

High-quality facilities are in place at the Distance Education Centre Victoria to produce television programmes and both audio-tapes and video-tapes. However, very large runs of tape duplication are contracted out. Face-to-face contact is brought about as far as possible through occasional seminars and excursions for senior secondary students, annual residential camps for junior secondary students, and, when possible, visits to the homes of full-time students by a team of teachers.

The telephone is thus a major means of communication between teachers and students. Telephones are used for direct calls and messages from students to teachers are recorded at the Distance Education Centre Victoria on an answering machine; as well, telephones are used for teleconferencing and fax transmissions. Student need is diverse, however, as they are scattered geographically, and some lack access to communications technology.

In Victoria, some of these developments have been considered or tested. Most interactive television programmes to date have been directed towards staff professional development and information. The Distance Education Centre Victoria is a major reception site for interactive television via satellite. Unfortunately, in Australia the reach of satellite television is limited, with relatively few households having access to it.

An electronic mail address is available to students who are comfortable with this medium of communication. Computer-assisted instruction, including computer-based training, multimedia, and artificial intelligence, has had limited use, although some progress has been made with developing materials in Hyper Card.

Computer-managed learning may be suitable for use in distance education, to manage and record the progress of learners through a course of study and to advise on learning actions. However, such issues as cost, access, and number of students in a given study area, and the use of an open-ended research approach requires consideration in connection with the extensive use of computer-managed learning. The importance of effective communication in a distance education operation cannot be overemphasised. In addition to the communication associated with the delivery of courses, a variety of other communications is necessary.

The third important component of open school instruction is face-to-face contact classes. These classes vary in length and number. In some open schools, for example, in Zambia, preference has been shown for conducting classes daily but for a shorter duration than in the conventional schools. In general, the argument is in favour of more contact classes for open schools than for open universities, as it is anticipated that open school students have less developed independent learning skills; therefore, they need greater supervision and direct instruction.

The kind of interaction that takes place in the face-to-face contact classes is also an issue. The open schools that prefer daily classes expect the teacher to cover the school curriculum in the contact sessions. Open school methods like self-study print material and electronic media supplement the tutor-based instruction, but tutor-based instruction remain the central strategy for learning delivery.

Another component of open learning instruction is student counselling. Counselling takes different shapes in different open schools. Wherever an open school offers a wide range of subjects, students need help in choosing the right combination of subjects, depending on their reasons for entering the open school. Similarly, student counselling is needed to monitor the progress of learning.

An equally important component of open schools is the mechanism for monitoring learning and providing help in self-assessments. Just as each instructional module provides in-text questions to monitor progress within the module, the open schools provide assignments and response sheets in each course. The open school student is expected to complete the assignment and submit it within a given time to the instructor, who in turn not only assesses but comments on the student's understanding of the material and suggests improvements.

The basic objective of student support services is to help students learn. Student support services have several components. The first component of student support is informing prospective students about the programmes and methods used at open schools. This "pre-student support" is particularly necessary to bring in suitable students. Targeted publicity is particularly important in developing countries, where electronic media are comparatively less developed.

The second component of student support relates to enrolment and registration. The open school may administer enrolment using a range of centralised and decentralised approaches. In some of the open schools, students enrol directly with headquarters—they send in their applications and course fees by mail. In other cases, the open school sets up regional schools or study centres and students enrol there.

A third component of student support is advice and counselling on selecting courses, particularly since open schools provide more and students are often not adequately prepared to choose in view of their own future goals.

The fourth component of student support is ensuring the timely availability of self-study print materials. Again several approaches have been adopted in delivering print materials. Most open schools mail the print materials to ensure delivery at each student's doorstep. However, postal services are costly and the time of delivery depends on the efficiency of the postal department in each country.

Some schools send the materials to the regional study centres by road and rail transportation and students collect the print materials there. This method is less expensive; but effectiveness again varies widely with the efficiency of the transportation system. The transportation system is used where open school students are concentrated geographically and regional study centres are within easy reach of the students, as in large cities; postal deliveries are used where students are dispersed geographically, as in rural areas, coastal zones, and remote areas.

Since much of the learning in open schools is based on self-study print materials, their distribution and timely availability to students is critical to the success of the open school. The fifth and most crucial component of student support services is personal contact programmes. They are largely used to supplement learning from the print material and electronic media, and include tutorials to answer questions, discussion sessions, and laboratory practicals and drills.

Since the learning skills are comparatively low among open school students compared to those in the open universities, open school students require longer exposure to direct teaching, greater attention, and more supervised self-study. Special care is needed in personal contact programmes to ensure that tutorials, interactive group learning, and laboratory practicals take place, not lectures. These components of student support services are interdependent and require integrated implementation.

Cost of Education

Open schools are often considered less expensive than conventional schools, but the reality is different. Similar to the conventional system, the cost of education is directly proportional to the quality of the programmes the open schools offer. However, open schools provide education to a larger number of students at the same cost and at comparable quality;

to that extent, they are cost effective. The principal cost in open schools is in the development, printing, and production of self-study print material; the quantity and quality of supporting material; the duration and level of personal contact classes; and the quality of teachers and instructors.

The costs decrease when calculated per student, when economies of scale are realised. The administrative overhead costs do not necessarily increase with expanded enrolment. Instead, the per-student cost of programme delivery remains more or less constant, except when very large volumes of learning materials are printed; in those cases, the unit cost of the print material is significantly reduced. An important point in the economics of open schools is that they require considerable investment at the beginning to set up the infrastructure and to start the processes of course development and materials design and production.

The unit cost of education in the initial years is, therefore, high. The actual cost of education varies widely between one country and another, depending on the level of enrolment as well as the type and quality of learning material. Few studies have been conducted on the cost of open schools. The lowest unit cost, as far as is known, is US$ 25, which covers all expenditures in the National Open School of India.

Most open universities have largely emerged out of government initiatives, but distance education in continuing and professional education have not. The nature of government support for open schools varies from one country to another and from one open school to another within the same country.

Unlike conventional schools, open schools are often only partially funded by government, which can vary from a token five to six per cent of recurring expenditure in India, to nearly total funding in British Columbia. Also governments provide relatively greater funding to open universities than to open schools. Similarly, the funding support by international and bilateral agencies also concentrates on open universities.

Management Issues

Open schools have already made a significant impact in all countries. They are now opening new vistas for the neo-literates, both adults and school dropouts, because of their flexibility and responsiveness to learning needs. In the fast changing socio-technological scene, retraining people for employment and at home is becoming a necessity, and open schools have considerable potential for contributing to general life enrichment as well as for retraining for employment.

Open schools have also been able to break down the barrier between vocational and academic schools— they place vocational courses on par with academic courses. From many considerations, open schools are capable of introducing a new dimension in education, which combines freedom to learn with functionality. In developed countries where conventional schools are well entrenched and have proven efficiency, open schools may emerge as a significant alternative to the conventional system.

However, the open school movement may be far more massive in the developing countries that are struggling to provide education to all in the face of a paucity of resources that forbids the lateral expansion of conventional schools and where the internal efficiency of the schools leaves much to be desired. Open schools in such countries, as can be seen from this collection of case studies, may be complementary and not an alternative school system.

The conventional and open school systems will grow together and continue to influence one another. Indeed, because of their pedagogical soundness, open schools may significantly influence the instructional processes in the conventional system. By their very nature and requirements, open schools must be location specific.

While there can be a few universal core principles, the development variable—whether a country's economy is developed or developing—determines the perspective and methods used in the open schools. Although access to education will be the common concern in developed countries, open schools provide greater choice of courses, where school instruction is available to every child.

In developing countries, open schools mean access to education for a larger number of people, with or without the freedom of choice. In some countries, open schools may be overrun by technology because of its availability and addiction to it, while others may resist technology despite its availability; others will not be able to afford technology. The common concern, however, will be to provide a pedagogically sound programme for students.

Open Schooling: Development in India

In the twenty-first century, information services play a dominant role in the promotion of lifelong learning. Pointing towards the future, the Indian National Policy on Education (1986) states that "the future thrust will be in the direction of open and distance learning." Open learning is thus expected to play an important role in India. Open learning was given a new impetus when the Open University in the United Kingdom was established in 1969; but other events have also aided the growth of open learning.

The de-schooling movement, as a precursor to open learning, represented a loss of faith in institutionalised learning. Radio, television, films, audiotapes, and computers had been used for some time, but only as supplementary material. By the 1970s, they were often integrated into the instructional system. This integrated use of radio and television (mass media) further promoted the growth of open learning. The need to design and adopt alternate strategies of education was a discernible trend on the international horizon in the 1960s. This concept of alternate education, taking education to the doorsteps of economically and geographically disadvantaged groups of students, ushered in the new era of open learning.

Independent India inherited a system of education that largely suited the needs of British colonial rule. The system was completely "bookish", memory-oriented, and elitist. Subject content, especially in language, history, and geography, was irrelevant to the Indian context. Science teaching was patchy and poor. Research facilities at the higher education level were practically nil. Approximately 4,000 high schools and 16 universities operated in the country. Sociologically, the institutional climate was authoritarian.

Teachers were respected by parents and feared by students. A socio-psychological gap existed between student and teacher. The textbook, the chalkboard, and the teacher were the tools of learning. The University Grants Commission was established in 1956. The Rural Institutes were also established in the same year by an order of the Government of India. Their aim was to nudge higher education in the direction of village and rural studies. The Indian Institutes of Technology were set up in phases.

The National Council of Educational Research and Training (NCERT), which accelerated educational change in India, came into being in 1961. NCERT's four constituent Regional Colleges of Education were established in 1962 and 1963. The scheme of correspondence education was included in the third five-year plan. An expert committee under the chairmanship of Dr. D. S. Kothari was appointed in 1960 to work out its details. The committee recommended correspondence courses in some selected universities, believing that they would reduce the pressure of student numbers, as well as reduce capital costs and possibly even the recurrent costs.

Correspondence education at the school level emerged in 1964 and 1965. The Conference of Boards of School Education (COBSE) recommended correspondence courses for private students, to improve academic standards. The Board of Secondary Education of Madhya Pradesh was the first to start correspondence courses in 1965, followed by Patrachar Vidyalaya, Delhi, and the Rajasthan Board of Secondary

Education, Ajmer, in 1968. The period from 1968 to 1988 was marked by developments in correspondence education, independent and part-time education, alternate education, and educational technology.

The use of satellites in education in India began in 1975 under the UNESCO-United Nations Development Programme project known as Satellite Instructional Television Experiment (SITE). The Indian Satellite (INSAT) for education was installed in orbit in 1984. The Centre for Educational Technology and State Educational Technology Units were upgraded into the Central Institute of Educational Technology (CIET) and State Institutes of Educational Technology (SIETs), respectively.

Thus, radio and television (mass media) began to play an important and supportive role in programmes specially for primary and adult education, and teacher training. In a way, "distance teaching" entered, if not altogether through the back door, then certainly not through the front door either. By 1985, fresh thinking about education had begun, resulting in the diagnostic exercise of educational maladies and the promulgation of the second National Policy on Education.

The new policy initiated several new educational schemes for enhancing both equity and the quality of education. Some of the better known schemes include: Operation Black Board for upgrading the quality of primary schools; District Institutes of Education and Training for pre-service and in-service training of primary and elementary school teachers; Navodaya Vidyalayas for talented rural children; the core curriculum; vocational education for secondary education; a rethinking of content and process at the primary and secondary levels; alternate education; adult education in the mission mode; academic staff colleges to train college and university teachers; and the open learning institutions at the university and school levels that lead to the establishment of Indira Gandhi National Open University (IGNOU).

Establishing the Open School project in 1979, Andhra Pradesh Open University in 1982, and later IGNOU and the National Open School (NOS) were structural innovations that promoted open, flexible, and responsive learning systems. Correspondence education had provided the student with the facility to study at his or her own pace. But it also had some limiting features. It adopted the same study scheme, syllabus, and examination system as the conventional schools.

The only difference was that correspondence students studied at a distance whereas the conventional students received face-to-face instruction. Freedom of location at which to study was the only freedom the correspondence system provided. It did not offer freedom in its eligibility requirements, duration of learning, choice of curriculum, or evaluation procedures. The idea of starting an open school surfaced in 1974.

During the International Conference on Correspondence Education held in New Delhi in 1978, the NCERT team benefited from the advice of international experts. Their suggestions greatly helped to conceptualise and set up the Open School in 1979 as a project school of the Central Board of Secondary Education. The concept of an open school at the secondary level was a big and bold departure from, and a considerable advance over the concept of correspondence education.

The aim was to liberate the system from its ingrained orthodoxy. Other considerations prompted the emergence of the open school as well. Financial constraints, family circumstances, or rigidities of the school system had caused many students to leave school long before they reached 14 years of age or completed the eighth grade.

The Open School was seen as a mechanism to give these early school leavers a second chance and to re-absorb them into the school system. In addition to the dropouts, many working adults, especially people working in the border security force, police, and railways keenly wanted to pass their matriculation in order to move upward in their jobs. The Open School gave them this opportunity. With its objectives and target student groups in mind, the Open School proposed four different programmes:

i) bridge, foundation, or preparatory courses;
ii) courses leading to secondary school examination;
iii) courses leading to senior secondary school examination; and
iv) technical, vocational, and life enrichment courses.

Within the first three years, the Open School made a mark and its success became widely known. Its fast growth and increasing popularity led to the establishment of the National Open School, which absorbed the Open School project in 1989. Open universities have been much praised all over the world; however, very few commendatory words have been said for open schools. One reason for this is that few open schools have been established in the developed world because most of these countries have compulsory secondary education and conventional schools to service their populations.

It is only in the developing world that the need for open schools is urgent, because they are an important structural innovation that will help provide education to all. Ensuring education for all is a vital concern of all developing countries; indeed, it is an overriding agenda item for nation building. Education for all includes basic education and is aimed at social and economic development, both for individuals and for nations.

Since the early 1950s, educational systems all the world over have begun "a process of expansion without precedence in human history". The situation in the developing countries is mixed. Massive expansion has often accompanied a lowering of educational standards and increasing inequalities in the scope of educational opportunities. Disparities are more acute in specific groups such as women, socially and economically disadvantaged students, and students with handicaps.

The Indian educational scene reflects the same trends. Despite an impressive expansion of educational facilities, the goal of education for all remains elusive. Even with the political will, overall enrolment in sixth grade is around 40 per cent. The situation is much more alarming in some states, including Bihar, Rajasthan, Madhya Pradesh, and Uttar Pradesh, where the enrolment of girls is around 20 per cent and the female literacy rate is about 15 per cent.

Since 1974, special efforts have been launched to improve educational access through the promotion of alternate education and the use of educational technology to spread and extend primary education. In India, the term basic education has an historical context and meaning. Basic education was Gandhi's concept and his wisdom resulted in a refreshing look at education. Gandhian basic education comprised:

i) the integrated teaching of various subjects like languages, science, mathematics, history, and geography;
ii) the integration of vocational education with academic learning;
iii) the inculcation of income-generation skills; and
iv) the development of a temper to promote dignity of labour.

Thus, the Gandhian basic education was seen as a system of education to develop an integrated human being who is self-supporting in skills; Swadeshi (nationalist) in outlook; respectful of the values of truth, simplicity, and non-violence; and aimed at the balanced development of head, heart, and hands. The connotation of the word basic in basic education for all is different. It means the basic skills and foundation knowledge that promote literacy, numeracy, and general awareness. Further, basic education for all also includes the development of certain values that are essential for human survival. Basic education for all includes:

i) literacy and numeracy;
ii) an elementary understanding of society and nature;

iii) a scientific outlook and a spirit of cooperation and tolerance;

iv) a positive attitude towards work, family, and community;

v) foundation skills for earning and living; and

vi) foundation skills and knowledge of citizenship.

This concept of basic education for all cuts across the boundaries of age and subject. It encompasses primary education as well as adult literacy and skill training. Its curriculum, therefore, is different from conventional primary education and is offered to students in all age groups.

Open learning in India, with its roots in the former correspondence education, was established to reduce the number of students that enrol in conventional universities and to make tertiary education less expensive. Elsewhere in the world, objectives were different. In England and Europe, open learning was established to promote adult vocational education.

In Canada and Australia, it was established to extend educational opportunities to students in sparsely populated areas. In the then Soviet Union, the focus was on vocational education. Although the government of India views open learning as a vehicle for achieving equity and social justice, it has had a rather slow start.

Each state open school should offer two types of courses: one related to school certificate courses and the other related to competency-based, non-certificate vocational courses. The first level of courses would provide primary and secondary education; the second would cater to basic, vocational, and needs-based education. School-level courses should have a strong component of primary education, which is especially relevant for grades five to eight, that is, the age group from 10 to 14 years old. Only a few schools keep their doors open to innovative practices. Selecting the most suitable head of the open school guarantees the success or failure of an institution. The head of the open school need not embody the virtues or a king among scholars or a topnotch researcher.

Optimal resources should be provided to open schools in the initial stage so that students from disadvantaged backgrounds can attain minimum levels of learning. International agencies like UNESCO can act as facilitators to promote open schools at the secondary level. By providing consultants to design and produce self-study materials, and by helping to revamp teacher education, they are welcome contributors.

In order to ensure quality education, teachers need special orientations in three areas: diagnostic testing; remedial teaching; and teaching to ensure the achievement of minimum levels of learning. These three concepts are interdependent and overlap. Teacher education programmes should be geared to inculcate skills on how to impart minimum levels of learning to primary students using diagnosis and remedial teaching.

In 1992, the National Policy on Education and Programme of Action were revised and the emphasis on mass education was strengthened. India currently welcomes investment in elementary education from several international and bilateral agencies, including the World Bank, the United Nations Development Programme, the Canadian International Development Agency, the European Community, and the United Kingdom Overseas Development Administration.

India is mobilising almost all of the resources available to solve the problem of illiteracy and to provide basic education before the twenty-first century. The National Open School must be seen from this changing point of view, linked to a new open economy and a restructured society. The National Open School mission aims to:

i) universalise education;
ii) increase social equity and justice; and
iii) develop a learning society.

Due to its social and national concerns, the National Open School must be seen as one of government's important instruments in the universalisation of education, and not as just another school. The National Policy on Education, 1986, as revised in 1992, recommended that "The National Open School will be strengthened and open learning facilities extended in a phased manner at the secondary level in all parts of the country."

The Programme of Action, 1992, emphasised both open vocational education and establishing meaningful links with workstations, industry, and other organisations. The Programme of Action also recommended that a National Consortium on Open Schooling be established and that the National Open School lead the consortium.

The eighth five-year plan document, which guides educational development from 1992 to 1996, made specific recommendations on open schools and established certain targets. The plan target was to provide additional enrolment for 600,000 students through open schooling. The plan also indicated the desirability and involvement of the open school system in the post-primary stage.

The E-9 Summit released the Delhi Declaration, which declared a Joint Initiative on Distance Education. It states:

> The nine countries have agreed to work in collaboration on a distance education initiative, both to enhance training of teachers and other personnel, and to better reach neo-literates and marginalised groups. The initiative will be tailored to the specific needs and traditions of each country, to enhance existing efforts and to make use of new technologies. In turn, relevant international agencies will be ready to support, facilitate, and coordinate such an initiative by undertaking assessment studies, by holding meetings, by capacity building modalities, and by seeking financial sources of support.

Figure 3.1 indicates three distinct roles for the National Open School:

i) an institution with strong post-literacy, elementary, secondary, senior secondary, vocational education, and continuing education programmes;

ii) a national leader, sfacilitating the establishment of state open schools, coordinating standards, and providing resource support to open schools; and

iii) an international interface, comprising programme delivery, human resource development, and other resource support to open schools in the Third World, and exporting education products for open schooling.

The National Open School has developed in three distinct phases. From 1979 to 1989, the institution operated as the "Open School"—a project of the Central Board of Secondary Education, which is an examining body for conventional secondary and senior secondary schools. As part of a conventional institution, the open school built a solid foundation of courses—the bridge, secondary, and senior secondary courses.

The most remarkable feature of the open school at this time was its flexibility, usually the characteristic of a single-mode open learning institution. As well, curriculum, self-instructional material, and a mechanism of programme delivery were designed, implemented, and refined during this period. From 1989 to 1992, the National Open School was established as an autonomous organisation by the Government of India. In November 1989, the open school project was subsumed into the National Open School, and a mechanism for examination and certification was established. In 1990, the Government of India authorised the National Open School to conduct examinations and act as the certifying authority at the secondary and senior secondary levels. As a result, it the function of a board of examination. Another initiative taken at this time was to provide open vocational education. From 1993 on, the National Open School shifted from "a school and board combined" to "a national institution of open learning". It envisioned itself as a state instrument providing education for all through open learning. This period is characterised by a search for a new identity as a national institution.

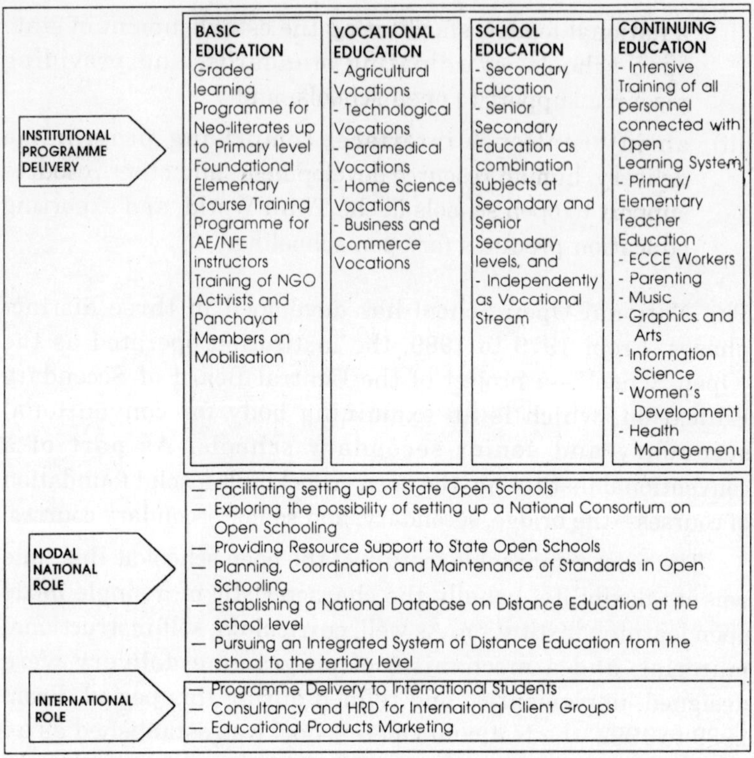

Figure 3.1: Systemic view of National Open School

Several innovative features distinguish the National Open School as an open learning institution. Flexibility and openness characterise these features, which include the following:

i) *No upper age limit*: Although the National Open School has a lower age limit of 14 years for entry into its courses, there is no upper age limit. Thus, more than 30 per cent of National Open School students are over the age of 20, with some students older than 50 years of age.

ii) *No rigid entry qualifications*: The National Open School expects a minimum level of competence for entry into its courses. Any student who has passed primary school can enrol in the bridge course or the secondary course. To enrol in the senior secondary course, however, a candidate must have a secondary pass certificate, to maintain equivalence with other examining bodies.

c) *Choice of courses*: Students may choose from a given list of subjects according to their individual interests, without restriction. For example, a senior secondary student may choose word processing, history, physics, accounting, and one language. Altogether, 26 subjects are offered in the secondary and senior secondary courses. Also the National Open School is developing more than 80 vocational and life enrichment courses, which students may combine with academic courses.

d) *Self-pacing*: Students are free to study at their own pace and have up to five years to complete a course of five subjects. Students may study one or more subjects at a time, and postpone studying for a while, if necessary, without seeking permission.

e) *Quality learning material*: Students are provided with semi-programmed interactive self-study learning materials, which have been developed by a team comprising some of the best teachers and writers available. The learning materials are written in simple language and are presented attractively, with access devices and built-in feedback to help the students.

f) *Media support*: Learning is supported, although marginally, by audio-tape and video-tape programmes in selected subjects and difficult topics. Some tapes are developed by the National Open School and others are purchased.

g) *Personal contact programmes*: The National Open School provides contact sessions, during which students can ask questions and seek guidance in their studies. Students can also view or listen to audio-tape and video-tape programmes or carry out practical assignments.

h) *Choice in taking examination time*: In order to make independent study more meaningful, the National Open School allows students to take examinations when they are ready. Examinations are held twice a year and students are free to choose not only which examinations, but also how many to write. Students are credited for every subject they pass. The credits are accumulated on computer, and, when sufficient credits have been obtained, a certificate is awarded.

The National Open School develops its own curriculum using a team approach. Curriculum in the National Open School has two major features. First, it is broadly based and intimately linked to life situations so that learning is in context. Second, it is interdisciplinary and cuts across the boundaries of specialised knowledge in favour of general education, which is the goal of the secondary school.

Like other distance education institutions, printed self-study learning materials play a major role in the teaching and learning process at the National Open School. Over the years, however, interaction with students has made it possible to make the learning package more effective. Accordingly, the National Open School learning materials comprise the following:

i) self-study print materials;.
ii) audio-tapes as an essential component in language courses and as support material in other subjects;
iii) concept maps;
iv) sample question papers;
v) assignments;
vi) charts and maps;
vii) study guides;
viii) glossaries;
ix) practical manuals; and
x) science laboratory kits.

The learning materials are developed by course teams, whose members are drawn from national and regional institutions like the National Council of Educational Research and Training (NCERT), the Technical Teachers Training Institutes, colleges, and universities, as well as from conventional schools. The self-study print materials are the mainstay of the learning package.

The major components of the self-study print materials include a concept map, an introduction, statement of objectives, presentation of contents in sections, in-text questions for self-check and feedback, a summary, the terminal exercises, and a set of assignments.

Even though the National Open School was established by the Ministry of Human Resource Development in the Government of India, it is registered as a society under the Society's Registration Act, and as such, is an autonomous organisation. But because the National Open School was set up and partly funded by the government, it is largely governed by Government of India rules, and, as a result, has only partial autonomy.

The highest statutory body in the National Open School is the General Body, which includes representatives from the Ministries of Human Resource Development, Personnel, and Information and Broadcasting, Door Darshan and All India Radio, the provincial governments, and an expert in each of the areas of distance education, women's development, technology, vocational education, media, and industry.

The National Open School is divided into three departments:

i) Academic,
ii) Examination, and
iii) Administration.

The Academic Department includes vocational education, media, student support services, the life enrichment and continuing education programme, basic education, and planning and evaluation, as well as the academic open secondary and senior secondary education. Similarly, the Administration Department includes publications, finance and accounts, material distribution, and admission, as well as normal administrative functions like personnel, purchasing, and maintenance.

The National Open School maintains a low per-unit cost of education. Student's fee account for 95 per cent of the cost of education. A secondary student pays the equivalent of US$ 21.70 for five courses, and a senior secondary student pays US$ 25.80. The students in exempted categories, including women, people with handicaps, and the socially disadvantaged, pay the equivalent of US$ 15 and US$ 19 for secondary and senior secondary courses, respectively.

One major challenge in building an institution is shifting the perspective of an institution among the academic staff and the senior administrators. This challenge was particularly pertinent in the National Open School, because it had to change from a school delivering purely education to a national institution with a larger role to play.

In other words, efforts were made to provide a new conceptual thrust—what the Indira Gandhi National Open University represents at the post-secondary level, the National Open School now represents at the school level. On the other hand, the National Open School also acts as the national resource agency for open schools in India, the way the National Council of Educational Research and Training supports the conventional school system.

Over the years, the National Open School has played a significant role in open secondary and senior secondary education. Its mission is the universalisation of education, greater equity, and social justice. This mission cannot be achieved unless open school programmes are made available in the mother tongue, through regional languages.

Currently, the National Open School offers its programmes only in English and Hindi, but a large number of potential students neither speak nor read Hindi or English. During 1993-94, a major initiative was taken to develop curriculum and learning materials in regional languages and to adapt the other subject material in nine regional languages. Significant progress has been made in four regional languages.

The qualitative development of open learning depends on multi-channel learning and, consequently, media play a significant role. During 1993-94, an initiative was taken to harness the educational potential of mass media. More than 20 curriculum-based video-tape programmes and four audio-tape programmes were developed or procured. The National Open School has been assigned the special role of coordinating and maintaining standards in open schools in India.

The school is expected to facilitate the set-up of state open schools, as well as to develop a consortium of open schools and an open school database. The initiative in rendering, adopting, and developing learning materials in regional languages is a preparatory step towards that end.

ODL CURRICULUM FOR TEACHERS

The term 'open and distance learning' is used as an umbrella term to cover educational approaches that reach teachers in their schools, provide learning resources for them, or enable them to qualify without attending college in person, or open up new opportunities for keeping uptodate no matter where or when they want to study. Open and distance learning often makes use of several different media. Students may learn through print, broadcasts, the internet and through occasional meetings with tutors and with other students.

The University of the South Pacific was one of the earliest users of communication satellites and is able to run two-way seminars with its students by means of satellite links. The university's early adoption of distance education has made good quality teacher education available that would have been beyond the resources of the individual small states of the Pacific.

The British Open University was set up in 1969 to widen access to education in Britain and has served as a model to many others. At the request of the government it introduced a programme for a certificate in education for graduates who wanted to enter teaching but had no professional qualification.

Teaching materials were distributed partly by mail and partly through the internet. Trainee teachers were based in schools where a mentor guided their teaching practice. Students used computer conferencing as an integral part of the course to interact with tutors and with each other. Open and distance learning may use print, broadcasts, cassette recordings, computer-based materials, computer interaction, videoconferencing, and face-to-face learning.

Open and distance learning is often seen as barely legitimate. Its history is marked by the work of institutions that accepted student fees, gave them poor service, and kept their costs down by encouraging students to drop out once they had paid all their money. Learning at a distance, particularly from printed materials, lends itself to rote learning. If teaching material gives all the answers then there is no room for an individual response while if it fails to do so the student may feel challenged but frustrated.

Distance learning can be a soulless and isolated activity so that dropping out is more attractive than going on. Most parents and probably most educational planners would encourage their own children to study at a conventional university rather than an open university.

Distance education has been powerfully effective in reaching audiences who could not meet their educational needs from conventional institutions. In Colombia, a radio-based school was, in the 1970s, reaching over 100,000 rural peasant students every year. The National Technological University in the United States is using satellite and broadcasting technology to meet the needs of engineers for postgraduate study without their having to leave their jobs and attend a campus.

In China, the combined use of television, classroom sessions, and printed materials is providing university education to about a third of all the students in higher education. A church-based nongovernment organisation, the American private sector, and the government authorities in China have all perceived distance education as legitimate because of its power to widen access to education.

Open and distance learning provides opportunities for student interaction with tutors, and it allows open-ended dialogue, often regarded as the touchstone of legitimate education. Thus, while open and distance learning may lend itself to rote learning—as does learning in large classrooms—this is not an essential or defining characteristic. Many programmes of teacher education, in all continents, have succeeded in enrolling students in significant numbers.

Where teachers have been promised improved status or pay at the end of the course, completion numbers can be as impressive as enrolment numbers. In the British Open University, completion rates appeared to be relatively high. In contrast, a programme in India had a completion rate of less than 20 per cent while about half the teachers learning about new communications technologies in Chile did not complete the course, partly because of difficulty in paying their fees.

Teacher education projects in Indonesia and Sri Lanka set out to measure learning gains and found reasonable evidence of effectiveness that is in line with the evidence on examination results. It would also be interesting to ask whether the students of trained teachers performed better than those of untrained but unfortunately we have limited evidence, and hardly any of it from open and distance learning.

The poorly qualified teachers are not much more effective than poor unqualified teachers and that there is therefore a case for improving—and spending more on—teacher education.

A study from the United States which compared student achievement and teacher policies within its states 'demonstrates that the states leading the nation in student achievement and those that have made the most significant gains in achievement are the states that have the most highly qualified teachers and that have made consistent investments in teachers' professional development.

There are number of broad-based comparisons have been made between conventional and distance-education approaches in terms of the cost per student or cost per successful student. Of course these comparisons are crude, and lump together very different kinds of distance-education programme.

Open and distance learning is often characterised as having high fixed and low variable costs which therefore allow for economies of scale: with more students the unit costs go down. The large teacher-education programmes in China, or the early programme in Tanzania, demonstrate this. In considering teacher education, however, other factors are often as important in determining comparative costs. If trainee teachers study part-time, with reduced periods of residence at a college then there are likely to be savings in the cost of residence and governments are less likely to pay an allowance while they are studying.

Furthermore, if trainees are teaching, either full or part-time, while they study, cost analysis needs to take account of the value of this work. Costing needs to take account of arrangements for student support and, often critical, of arrangements for classroom teaching and its supervision.

The evidence shows that distance education, in its various forms, can work and if well-designed can be educationally legitimate. It has been applied to the education of teachers and has been shown to be effective on a number of measures. In terms of cost per student, distance education programmes have often shown advantages over conventional programmes.

Distance education been used to teach, support and develop teachers for many years. Since then open and distance learning has been used in many countries of the world with a reasonable record of success. The use of new information and communication technologies has drawn new attention to open and distance learning and offers new possibilities. In some high population countries such as China and Pakistan, distance programmes have played an essential role in providing teacher education on a huge scale.

In many Latin American countries distance education has been used widely to support curriculum reform and teacher upgrading. Teacher education by distance is being used to redress inequalities in teaching qualifications in post-colonial Namibia and Zimbabwe and in South Africa, as a tool for reconstruction of the teaching service in Uganda. In other countries, it is being used to reach marginalised communities such as refugees in Sudan, itinerant communities in Mongolia, and minority groups in northern Pakistan.

Using distance education for teacher training has various potential advantages. Large programmes have brought economies of scale. In contrast to college-based training, distance programmes can provide access to courses on a much larger scale and wider geographical reach. It can overcome regional differences in access to teacher education. It provides a means of sidestepping the slowness and dilution of the cascade approach.

In continuing professional development, distance education can help avoid the cost of replacing a teacher who has gone to full-time education. It can open up access to teacher-training opportunities for teachers with family responsibilities who are earning an income and need to remain within their communities. The establishment of a decentralised distance education structure can also be used to support training in the districts and serve as a basis for the development of a programme for the continuing development of teachers.

In print-poor countries, self-study materials can become a permanent resource. It can also 'put information about curricula and teaching approaches directly into the hands of individual teachers' and cut down the time between learning about new teaching practices and trying them out in the classroom. This is particularly important in curriculum reform and short professional development courses.

Carefully balanced mixed-mode teaching can help to double and triple a college's training output per year. Where the infrastructure for them is in place, new information and communication technologies have opened up a range of new opportunities for course- and resource-based learning in teacher education. Three general points need to be stressed.

First, distance education is of potential benefit to teachers because it can reach scattered populations and can offer them education and training without their having to leave their schools. Its has great logistical advantages. This means that it offers the chance of accelerating the supply, or the updating of teachers, beyond what could be done through conventional means. Second, good programmes of open and distance learning have benefited from its strengths and avoided its weaknesses. Some aspects of teacher education need to be done face-to-face, or need close interaction with a tutor or with other students. Others do not. Programmes that combine conventional and distance methods are likely to be better than those that rely on a single approach.

Third, and for that reason, the more successful programmes have been carefully integrated into the structure of teacher education as a whole. They have not been designed as second-class alternatives to conventional education but as a part of a complementary system using a variety of different approaches, each chosen for its appropriateness to the curriculum and the audience.

There are four elements of the teacher's curriculum:

i) general education,
ii) subject knowledge,
iii) pedagogy, and
iv) practical teaching.

All of these elements have been addressed in different programmes of distance education, using a variety of technologies. Distance education would seem to lend itself to the first element; there is wide experience of using open and distance learning methods for the traditional curriculum of secondary or tertiary education and a wealth of experience in offering an effective equivalent curriculum of this kind.

In many countries there are teachers, or student teachers, with quite limited background education. Often these are the older and more remote teachers for whom open and distance learning may be a more convenient method of study than conventional education. Using open and distance learning to raise the level of their general education may be a simple and effective means of raising the quality of the teaching force. Extending teachers' knowledge of the subjects they are to teach may be more demanding if it is asking teachers both to acquire new subject knowledge and at the same time to think about how they are to present it in the classroom.

In Guyana, for example, a teacher training project dealt with this by running initial, pre-training programmes designed to increases the academic competence of unqualified primary and junior secondary teachers in English, mathematics and science in order to get them to the level needed for entry to a conventional teachers' college. Educators have also used distance-education approaches to bring new thinking and teaching practice about specific subjects of the curriculum.

In Latin America regional collaborative projects have been set up in environmental education, mathematics and science. Some aspects of pedagogy or of child development lend themselves well to open and distance learning. Video examples of real-life classroom teaching in a variety of contexts can give teachers a wider range of exemplary approaches than would be possible in conventional face-to-face learning.

Initial teacher education and training is the programme of studies which leads to qualified teacher status according to the official standards of a country. It is the basic or first level of qualification for a teacher. It may be taken as a pre-service programme or an in-service one. Continuing professional development enables teachers to extend existing knowledge and skills and develop new ones. Some of this takes the form of long structured courses leading to formal qualifications.

In some countries, qualified and unqualified teachers alike participate in continuing professional development. It may be provided as in-service activities (on-the-job learning) or out-of-school courses of varying length (off-the-job or in vacations). In general, distance-education programmes have been developed with varied intentions: of widening access to teaching qualifications; of disseminating good practice; of strengthening the education system as a whole by reaching not only teachers but the wider community; in enabling school-based training and professional development and as a means of strengthening the links between theory and practice, focusing on the school as a site of teachers' learning.

Some countries have used distance education to provide a route to initial qualifications for significant numbers of teachers, both new entrants to teaching and experienced unqualified teachers. Distance education is therefore also being used to raise the skills, deepen the understanding and extend the knowledge of teachers. Some programmes are broadly focused while others are targeted at specialist groups. Programmes are taken either by individuals or by groups of teachers who are encouraged to participate by their schools or their employers.

For example, a non-profit television station is taking the lead on supporting school groups in Brazil. In other cases, programmes are available for individual teachers who want to improve their skills and their status, often enrolling on an individual basis, and at their own expense. The Indira Gandhi National Open University in India has a number of programmes of this kind. In both England and Pakistan, for example, ministries of education have called on national open universities to distribute information and training on new curricula, rather than attempt to bring teachers together for this purpose. Some programmes using mass media have also sought to widen the audience beyond the core target of teachers to the broader community.

Distance education can have a role in programmes of curriculum reform which the aim to change either the content or the process of education. In South Africa, the Open Learning Systems Educational Trust is using the radio to improve the teaching of English, and to support teachers in this work. The OLSET programme in South Africa has been effective in reaching large numbers of teachers not only with prescription and advice on how to teach English as a second language but with well-designed lessons, provision of models, guidance in using the radio or audio-cassette resources and support for changes in teaching methods.

Distance education has been used for teachers' career development. As they seek promotion, or aim for the next qualification level, or aspire to become a headteacher, or work in a teachers' college, or become an inspector, teachers need to acquire new skills. A multinational distance education project in West Africa has developed a training programme in school management for headteachers and aspiring heads.

In brief, open and distance learning has been widely applied to teacher education and there is some record of success in its use for all four regular elements of the curriculum—general education, subject-specific knowledge, pedagogy, and practical teaching. With differing emphases on different parts of the curriculum it has been deployed for teachers at different stages of their careers, and in support of national programmes of development and of curriculum reform.

The history of distance education is littered with projects that looked good initially but could not be sustained as they were not built into national educational systems. Decisions about such issues as the allocation of government resources, the recognition of qualifications, or the use of teachers college facilities or staff are all likely to have implications for the educational service as a whole. Some of the planning choices within open and distance learning will affect people outside a ministry of education: teachers' associations and unions will be interested in the conditions of service for teachers working in a new role; broadcasting agencies, asked to transmit broadcasting materials, will certainly have a view about the timing of broadcasts and may want a measure of influence or even control over their content.

The most successful programmes are those where open and distance learning is closely integrated with other approaches to education and professional development. The planning of open and distance learning may involve policy issues at international, national and institutional level. The international issues arise in part because the forces of globalisation are affecting the content and practices of education, in part because new policy issues arise when education is no longer confined within national frontiers.

Programme planners are thus increasingly exposed to innovations in teacher education and need to make judgements about the desirability, feasibility and acceptability of these internationalised ideas within their country and programme. Changes to more practice-based teaching education, for example, have been encouraged internationally and become part of the common discourse about education.

International conventions on the role and status of teachers as agents of change naturally affect national policy. At the same time, educational cooperation across borders, and cross-border enrolment, put on to the decision maker's agenda jurisdictional questions about cross-cultural transference and language and about the control of cross-border enrolment and its accreditation or recognition.

Political, economic, technical and regulatory issues concern the respective roles of the private and public sector; educational institutions are likely to seek access to telecommunications on favourable terms, possibly through the use of governments' regulatory powers in the telecommunications sector, or may want more freedom to use telecommunications than has traditionally been available. Within the education sector, decisions about such issues as the allocation of resources, fee policies, the recognition of qualifications, the regulating and monitoring systems needed or the use of teachers college facilities or staff are all likely to have implications for the educational service as a whole.

For institutions changing to dual-mode status, a key issue will be the balancing of resources allocated to open and distance learning against those of conventional provision and the systematic planning of policies to manage institutional change effectively. This is likely to include new faculty policies (new contractual and workload agreements, training, renegotiation of union contracts, evaluation and support); student policy issues (materials delivery, library access, counselling, financial aid, registration and record-keeping, technical support) and legal policy development (intellectual property including ownership of materials, copyright, and faculty, student and institutional liability).

In open and distance learning functions are divided between different sections of the same organisation, or between different organisation. Where a project or programme is to enrol, advise, teach and examine students it needs structures for a set of different functions. To make distance education work you need structures and facilities for:

i) governance, planning, management and funding
ii) materials development and production
iii) materials reproduction and distribution
iv) student recruitment and advice
v) student support including the supervision of classroom practice
vi) assessment and evaluation of learners
vii) feedback system/formative evaluation
viii) record systems.

Any organisation needs a governance structure that will make major policy decisions; arrangements of planning, management and funding are likely to be the responsibility partly of people working within a distance teaching institution and partly of people outside. The development of teaching materials—or their acquisition from outside—is a basic function: distance education depends on such materials. They may be developed in-house, or by external course writers, and are likely to be in a variety of media.

An institution will need not only writers but people who can edit materials, so that they work effectively at a distance, and people to brief and train writers and editors. Materials then need to be reproduced, if they are in the form of print or cassettes or CD-ROMs and distributed. Broadcasting or videoconferencing also demand a distribution function of a different kind. Structures and systems are needed to recruit students and advise them about the programme.

Most students needs support, guidance, and feedback on their work. Where teacher education programmes include a practical element, concerned with their competence or skills in the classroom, arrangements are also needed to supervise this. Then, in many programmes students need to be assessed and their work examined or evaluated. A feedback system on the work of the institution or programme as a whole is needed to provide checks on how well it is working while a record system, important for any form of education, is indispensable where students are dispersed, needs to be designed and maintained.

Then there are many examples in which prime responsibility rests with a teachers college. Most often this has meant that a college, which is already teaching conventionally, acquire new responsibilities for teaching at a distance. At the outset, however, a teachers college which is beginning distance education needs to develop skills—in material development, for example—that its staff do not already possess. Universities have also been called on to play a role here. They may have two areas of expertise: in teacher education where they have a faculty of education and in open and distance learning.

Using a university for teacher education makes it possible to take advantage of structures and systems that are already in place. There may, however, be problems of fit and adjustment if a university has no experience, in, say, the education of primary school teachers which has generally been the responsibility of non-university teachers colleges. There have also often been practical difficulties within dual-mode universities in the almost indispensable job of developing materials.

In some institutions, the capacity of a central distance education unit may be purely administrative. In others, it has overall responsibility for the pedagogical quality of distance education materials, and for staff training. All of these variations in university practice will have a bearing on the skills that can be deployed by a university in a teacher education programme. Universities have run programmes of two kinds which, oversimplifying, can be described as supply-led and demand-led.

In some instances ministries of education have turned to a university to run a national programme because it has the infrastructure for materials development and distribution. In other cases, a university has developed courses, especially for continuing professional development, because it is itself aware of a demand from teachers that will help their professional development. The Indira Gandhi National Open University in India, for example, runs programmes on which students enrol individually, paying their own fees, in order to raise the level of their qualifications.

If there is an existing open university, or a university with a distance-teaching department, it may make sense to use their infrastructure rather than creating something new. Sometimes, there are also advantages to bypassing the traditional system in an attempt to be free from its political or pedagogical constraints, or its inertia.

Cooperation with local colleges of education may be necessary for the supervision and management of the practical side of teacher education. In practice, the whole organisation and balance of the course components is dependent on local conditions and can, therefore, vary considerably in quality. During the college-based phase, teaching practice is assessed by teaching college tutors while in the distance phase, trainees are assessed by the host school's headmaster four times a week, regional supervisors twice a term and college tutors five times during 20 months.

Programmes which appear to have been most successful at achieving effective articulation and channels of communication are those that are very systematic in their planning and spend time, ahead of implementation, in identifying needs, on the basis of consultation and among a wide range of stakeholders. This seems to be symptomatic of distance-education programmes and initiatives which have been freed from a pressing imperative of going to scale; which, instead, have recognised the importance of building up a consolidated base as a prerequisite for effective delivery.

In India, for example, a district-based programme for the development of primary education has used open and distance learning alongside other methods of teacher education. It has combined strong decentralised decision making and management with unequivocal support, if not direction, from the ministry. This support has opened up access to existing state teacher education structures, resources and channels of communication at different national, state and local levels.

The increasing international attention with the development of e-learning and the promise that internet-based teaching will share the world's educational resources and make distance education more widely available than ever before, while there have been a handful of programmes that use the new technologies to deliver teaching across frontiers. In exploring the possibilities for international cooperation the planner will want to define the terms of the cooperation and is then likely to be guided by seeking a balance between the quality and economy that may be achieved by the use of external resources and the need for teacher education to match its national or local culture.

There are increasingly important regional developments in open and distance learning. Within the European Union, the European Commission has encouraged cooperation in all areas of education through open and distance learning and the use of the new technologies. In southern Africa, there is a long history of cooperation, including the cooperative development of teaching materials for distance education.

The effective management of open and distance learning demands some central management of planning so that materials development, production and distribution is often run from the centre; student recruitment and some student support may often rest there. Collaborative arrangements are most often needed for the supervision of classroom practice and for accreditation.

Collaboration tends to be difficult and demands links at various levels within the organisations for smooth running and the resolution of conflicts. The links may be particularly difficult to articulate in large, federal, countries where resources may be needed at federal, provincial and district level. Teachers associations and unions have a role to play both in planning and in considering the effects of teacher-education programmes on their members' conditions of service and opportunities for professional advancement.

Role of Techologies

Within teacher education, the new technologies have been used for two different purposes. One is training teachers to learn about information and communication technologies and their use in teaching as computers are introduced to schools. In many countries this is being done through face-to-face training programmes, often as part of initial teacher education. Some countries have developed policies which require all initial teacher education programmes to include compulsory courses in the technologies as a strategy for building capacity in relation to them.

The other role of information and communication technologies is as a means of providing teacher education, either as a core or main component of a programme or playing a supplementary role within it. Teachers colleges are beginning to experiment with the use of computer-based material to strengthen and broaden their curriculum. The development of teachers' capacity in using the technologies cannot happen in isolation. Plans need to take account of the use of the technologies elsewhere in the education system and in the wider environment.

The technologies necessitate an appropriate technical infrastructure and funding to support it. If the use of the technologies is seen as a function of teachers generally, this needs to be reflected in national policies and strategies and in the curriculum for both initial teacher education and continuing professional development. While teacher educators are a key element in establishing the use of information and communication technologies in education, many teacher educators themselves lack skills and training in the use of the technologies or opportunities to apply and develop their knowledge and skills.

OLSET in South Africa has used radio for schools, at a modest cost per learner, because it is a relatively large country, using broadcasts in a single country, and with a national infrastructure that means many schools can use radio. In contrast, computer-based learning would not be realistic for its many rural schools.

The actual costs of a particular technology will depend on local circumstances and it is not possible to set out an international set of standard prices. Even within a single medium or technology costs can vary widely: sophisticated television documentaries have far higher production costs than teaching programmes which consist of a talking head and the equivalent of a blackboard.

American research has indicated a very wide range of costs for preparing material that is presented by computer, with the lowest where this is simply using the computer to present print and the highest where designers move into simulations or virtual reality. The beginning experience of online tutoring suggests that the costs of this may put strains either on budgets or on tutors' workloads, mainly because there is no ready way of controlling the time tutors spend responding to their students or the demands that students put on their tutors.

If there is a computer conference, tutors may feel a responsibility to monitor its contents, regardless of the length of material placed there by students. Where students can contact their tutor by email, they tend to demand more of their tutors' time than when they are submitting a conventional assignment. In the absence of good cost studies of online teaching the only advice for the planner is to welcome the pedagogic advantage of being able to have ready contact with distant students while seeking a way of containing the costs.

Much education, at primary, secondary and tertiary levels has conventionally been funded by government and government funding has been the norm for many programmes of initial teacher education and training. Many governments have been willing to fund not only initial teacher education but some programmes of continuing professional development, especially for curriculum reform or for some upgrading programmes in countries trying to raise the minimum standard of teacher qualification.

Teachers are, however, often expected to pay fees where they enrol on a course of continuing professional development which will benefit them in terms of career advancement or salary increment. Some parts of a programme may be funded by government but not through a ministry of education. If education can get access to state broadcasting time and facilities, at a nominal charge or free of cost, then broadcasting transmission costs do not fall on the ministry of education budget.

In some jurisdictions there may be an expectation that government should meet the full costs of teacher education because of its importance for the quality of the education service as a whole. The imposition of student fees may hold down enrolment, discourage students, and is likely to be socially regressive.

The freedom of action and non-bureaucratic structure that marks effective nongovernment organisations has to be balanced against difficulties they may face in integrating their work with regular state activity and ensuring its sustainability. External finance from funding agencies may also present problems of sustainability. Many funding agencies have been willing to meet capital costs, and to fund pilot projects, but expect governments to meet recurrent and continuing costs.

Course development has sometimes, but not always, been treated as capital expenditure even though its major cost element is likely to be for staff time. The trade-off is often between initial freedom of action, bought with external funds, and long-term integration and sustainability. While open and distance learning does not require the building of colleges and halls of residence, it does require some capital investment, for the development of systems and materials, well in advance of student recruitment.

Costs are likely to be incurred for initial planning, development of materials, their reproduction and distribution, their reception, student support, training and capacity building, and maintenance. There are costs associated with initial planning and initiation of teacher education at a distance, even if these amount only to the use of existing capacity within the educational system. These costs have often been found from regular government budgets.

Difficulties can arise where teachers or trainers are already in government employment, working in education, but asked to develop materials as an extra or different job. In some cases regulations do not allow them to be paid extra; in others sanctions are impossible if they do not deliver the material.

Strategies need to be put in place that allow for the effective development and editing of material that is fair to staff and ensures materials are delivered on time.

Funds for writers are not enough: editing of materials, to ensure their educational effectiveness and get them to camera-ready state or undertake desktop publishing, is likely to cost as much as their initial writing. The costs for reproducing and distributing teaching materials may fall in various places. If material is broadcast, transmission costs may be met by the broadcasting agency. If learners have to collect materials, some of the costs of distribution fall on them.

Where materials are distributed electronically then, once the capital investment has been made, costs to the initiating institution may be negligible. Costs for reception of materials for an individual learner often fall on the learner, who may be expected to have a radio or, in an industrialised country, to obtain a computer. Where the distance-teaching system brings learners together there may be costs for the development or supply of specialist centres or equipment or negotiations for their use by learners. There will always be costs for the continuing support of students and arrangement for supervision of their classroom practice.

Funds will be needed for training and capacity building, especially as an unfamiliar project is being set up. As with initiation costs, this is an area where funds have often been obtained both from government and from external agencies. These are not, however, once-for-all costs: just as we argued for continuing professional development as an aim of teacher education so it will be necessary for those working in a specialist open and distance learning institution. Funding is not a once-off activity: maintenance of the whole system, of any equipment, and of teaching materials all incur costs.

The costs of maintaining teaching materials, in particular, are often underestimated at the outset: the effort needed to get them created the first time diverts attention from setting up a programme of continuing revision, improvement and updating.

Distance education for teachers has a patchy record, with many programmes started but abandoned, often because short-term funding arrangements could not be sustained. Open and distance learning has a potential advantage in terms of integrating theory and practice where it enables practising teachers to raise their skills by study at a distance and it is worth seeking strategies that will maximise that advantage. Conventional as well as distance-education programmes have, with varying success, confronted this need to turn what teachers know and believe into what they do to support children's learning.

Many conventional programmes fail to attend to this and some produce teachers who are formally qualified but have had only a token or minimal supervised school experience. In some countries, practical teaching forms no part of the final assessment of teachers. The issues for a distance-education provider are about managing the supervision and assessment of students in distant locations and how to design materials and activities in ways which integrate knowledge or theory with practice.

The way that distance education disperses responsibility for a programme among a range of partners, sometimes on a large scale over distance—for student support, administration, tutoring, course production, delivery and assessment-presents a number of logistical and methodological challenges for researchers. In many countries it is hampered by limited research capacity and expertise, limited research culture, and limited funding. Funding may be the key: education spends less on research and evaluation than many other areas of human enterprise.

Formative evaluation is likely to strengthen any educational institution. It has a particular significance for open and distance learning partly because its methods are complex and likely to involve many partners and partly because its students are distant, unseen, and often unheard. It is therefore necessary to build measures for quality assessment into all the processes of a distance-teaching institution.

Of the other areas, distance-teaching institutions have been particularly concerned to create appropriate systems to monitor system design, the development of teaching materials, and student support. In assessing alternative proposals for system design it is necessary to examine how open and distance learning articulates with the rest of the educational system so that it provides a quality of education that matches the needs of students which is recognised as being on par with conventional education.

There is now an extensive literature on the development of effective teaching materials for open and distance learning, in a range of different media, and a measure of agreement on the principles that underlie good instructional design. In designing an assessment system it is therefore appropriate to build in checks on the development and presentation of materials to ensure that they are pedagogically effective. Where teachers, studying at a distance, have themselves little experience as adult learners, or of learning outside a conventional classroom, they are likely to need considerable support, offered through written comments on assignments, or electronically, or through face-to-face contact with tutors.

Formative evaluation needs to provide information about the quality of open and distance learning generally, about the quality of the processes of a distance teaching institution, and about the assessment of individual teachers.

REFERENCES

Arnsten R. and A. Sheddick, *Accessing Experiential Learning through Collaborative Multimedia Learning Processes*, ICEL Conference, Cape town, S. Africa, July, 1996.

Jenkins, J., S., Inquai, T. Dodds, and D., Warr, "Distance teaching: A catalyst for curricular change for introducing vocational subjects", *ERIC document*: ED 280984, 1986.

Martin, B. L., "Using Distance Education to Teach Instructional Design to Preservice Teachers", *Educational Technology*, Vol. XXXIV, No. 3, March 1994.

Miller, G., "Technology, the curriculum and the learner: Opportunities for open and distance education", In R. Mills and A. Tait (eds.), *Supporting the learner in open and distance learning*, London, Pitman, 1996.

Mills, R. and A. Tait (eds.), *Supporting the Learner in Open and Distance Learning*, London, Pitman, 1996.

Mukhopadhyay, Marmar and Susan Phillips (eds.), *Open Scholing: Selected Experiences*, The Commonwealth of Learning, Vancouver, 1994.

Osberg, K. M., Virtual reality and education: where imagination and experience meet, *VR in the Schools*, 1995.

Perraton, H. (ed.), *Distance Education for Teacher Training*, London and New York: Routledge, 1993.

Ravitch, D., "Technology and the curriculum", in M.A. White (ed.), *What curriculum for the information age*? Hillsdale, NJ: Lawrence Erlbaum Associates, Inc., 1987.

Tait, A., "Planning Student Support in Open and Distance Learning", in *Open Learning*, 15 (3), 287-300, 2000.

UNESCO, *Teacher Education through Distance Learning, Technology, Curriculum, Evaluation,* Cost, Paris: UNESCO, 2001.

_______________ , *Analytical Survey, Distance Education for the Information Society, Policies, Pedagogy and Professional Development,* UNESCO Institute for Information Technologies in Education, Moscow: UNESCO/IITE, 2000.

4

Assessment of Open and Distance Learning

The digital technologies have enabled the connection of all participants in the teaching process (teachers, students, school) in a unique virtual school regardless of the geographical distances. With the help of multimedia computers, web schools, internet schools or virtual classrooms become the venue of organised and systematic acquisition of knowledge and perfectionisation. The development of open and distance learning is going in two directions:

i) education of adults, perfectioning, vocational re-training, specialisation and sub-specialisation
ii) acquisition of academic degrees at universities and academies or in higher education

The purpose of assessment and evaluation of students in open and distance learning does not only aim at evaluating acquired knowledge but also at detecting possible problems in the learning of the material. Thus the timely and direct help for the student is provided, which can result in higher motivation on the part of students. Teachers and leaders of the process of distance education must supervise the student and evaluate him appropriately in order to simultaneously evaluate the quality of educational material, contribute to their develpment and find the most efficient way of their presentation.

The assessment of students in the process of distance learning includes:

i) assessment of students' progress in the learning of educational materials
ii) assessment of the use of Internet communication services
iii) assessment of approach to educational materials.

Several kinds of tests or their combinations are used in open and distance learning:

i) time-limited/unlimited tests
ii) interactive tests.

The interactive type of tests enables the student after he has finished the test to obtain the results and to evaluate answers by means of statistic data. Such a form of test enables the student to check the acquired knowledge and get an insight to what extent he has understood the educational material. The use of time-unlimited tests enables students to return to parts of teaching materials with explanations in the process of test writing. It is possible to use time-limited tests if we want to check the acquired knowledge. Those tests do not allow the checking of correct answers while doing the exercises. This kind of tests provides a better insight into acquired knowledge.

Most teachers usually use tests that they can correct themselves, using also open-type questions, in an effort to create a better and more intimate communication with their students. On the basis of interactive tests, students' papers, use of communication services, students' motivation, final work and essays, teachres can make the final evaluation of students' work. By supervising the student during the teaching process we can make the final evaluation of the success of the teaching process and student's knowledge.

The most important feature of the virtual classroom is the communication between the student and the teacher, as well as among students themselves. Communication services make the basic frame for distance learning.

Communication within the distance learning is done by means of communication services: e-mail, internet telephone, desktop videoconferencing system, chat service, bulletin boards, newsgroups, white board, etc. The diversity of communication services and their possibilities facilitate a better presentation of educational material, but also the building of positive atmosphere in the school. The use of all communcation services requires a high degree of familiarity with internet technologies both on the part of students and teachers. It is very important whether students use communication services, i.e., whether they participate in the activities of the school, and how long and how well they do it.

The assessment of use of communication services allows the creation of an image of every student, his motivation, aspiration and understanding of educational material. The term assessment of access includes the assessment of the time of access, duration of work on certain materials, return to them, etc. It would be logical to suppose that students' return to teaching materials can mean revision of material, but it can also indicate certain unclear issues, possible problems, etc. If the student only superficially goes through the teaching materials we can also expect poorer results in tests, students' works or joint students' activities.

The assessment of access to educational materials and the use of communication services are offered almost by all open and distance learning (ODL) institutions. By processing log files it is possible to successfully plan consequent developments in the school but also have an insight in the work of each individual student. The assessment and evaluation of students' participation, acquisition of knowledge, habits and skills by means of ODL is not a simple process and it does not consist only of the check of knowledge after respective teaching units or at the end of teaching materials.

Historically, the precursor of ODL was correspondence education, which started in Europe and the United States in the mid nineteenth century. Beginning in the middle of the twentieth century and continuing today, television began playing a role in providing ODL courses and programmes. The continued and growing need for remote access to learning opportunities, linked with newer information systems and communication technologies, especially the use of the world wide web, has now pushed ODL into the centre of the discussion of educational practice in higher education.

According to a report by International Data Corporation, in 2002 approximately 85 per cent of two and four-year colleges were now offering distance education courses. Student enrolments were estimated to be over 2.2 million students, or 15 per cent of all higher education students. Investment in distance education was estimated to reach $2 billion dollar by the year 2003. Though the growth of open and ODL is noted as a significant feature in the current higher education environment, educators are not of one mind about distance learning.

The key factor is establishing the right mix of teaching modalities that includes instructor-led teaching, as well as computer and multimedia-based learning opportunities. Some educators express concern that the quality of education for students declines in the distance learning environment. Some teachers lack a coherent understanding of ODL practice and the full range of instructional design possibilities available to them in a distance learning environment to achieve desired outcomes.

Some major ODL initiatives emphasise educational issues only when related to fiscal implications of ODL efforts. Educators have an unprecedented opportunity to provide leadership and direction in helping to make sense of the confused ODL environment. The internal environment of higher education can be characterised as one that is oriented toward maintaining long-term stability. Higher education institutions are also characterised by conservatism and resistance to change. They respond slowly to the need to adapt to new imperatives.

The public perception and expectation about what goes on inside higher education has not changed either. These perceptions still largely revolve around the spatially located collegiate experience with closeness to faculty and fellow students being at its core. The external environment, on the other hand, can be described as a world in which the pace and complexity of change are overwhelming, and in which boundaries of time, geography and language no longer exist.

Educators are no longer dealing only with traditional students in terms of goals, age and residential status. Many students have extremely focused work related goals, are older, and are not interested in a residential experience. As a result of changing student perceptions, institutions must respond to an increasing diverse set of expectations.

ODL encompasses essentially all learning technologies, including "postal distribution, video broadcast, CD-ROM and web delivery" in which "instruction and learning interactions may take place independent of the relative physical locations of the individual participants." This definition may seem straightforward enough, but conceptual confusion is continually created with the advent of new terminology (i.e., distance learning, distributed learning, open learning, e-learning, flexible learning, learning portal and virtual classrooms). In addition, ODL borrows and leverages terminology from other disciplines, including psychology, sociology, philosophy, history, economics, organisational theory, adult education, general education and information technology.

ODL is a derivative field of adult education, which in itself is a "professionalising vocation", not a discipline in its own right. Other characteristics of ODL are following:

i) The influence of an educational organisation both in planning and preparation of learning materials and in the provision of student support services.

ii) The use of technical media, print, audio, video or computer to unite teaching and learner and carry the content of the course.

iii) The provision of two-way communication so that the student may benefit or even initiate dialogue. This characteristic distinguishes ODL from other uses of technology in education.

iv) The quasi-permanent separation of the learning group throughout the length of the learning so that people are usually taught as individuals and not in groups, with the possibility of occasional meeting for both didactic and socialisation purposes. ODL have identified four elements common to all distance learning experiences:

   a) The separation of teacher and learner during at least a majority of the instructional process.

   b) The influence of an educational organisation, including the provision of student evaluation.

   c) The use of educational media to unite teacher and learner and carry course content.

   d) The provision of two-way communication between teacher, or mentor, or educational agency and learner.

Globalisation has inspired additional ways of looking at ODL. Learning is the act or process of acquiring knowledge or skill. The ideal concept of open education would take the form of education permanent, open to all people at all levels, cradle-to-grave.

Students study independently and at a pace of their own choosing. The distinction between distance learning and open learning has been that as it evolved, distance learning incorporated technological advances into the teaching/learning process, whereas open learning did not necessarily do the same. The growth of "open" universities, most of which offer education at a distance, has not helped to clarify the distinction between the two.

The term open generally refers to institutions, such as the British Open University and many American community colleges, which have open admission policies. An open admissions policy is not necessarily a characteristic of distance learning programmes. Technological development is increasing the range of such media and increasing the way in which media can be combined.

For example, content management software on the web can be used to post syllabuses in combination with a synchronously delivered course via room videoconferencing. Transactional distance is a "distance of understandings and perceptions [not of geography] that may lead to a communication gap or a psychological distance between participants in the teaching-learning situation."

As a continuous variable, the magnitude of transactional distance is dependent upon "dialogue"—the potential for communication between learner and instructor, and "structure"—the degree to which a learning programme can be individualised for specific learner needs. Learners operating at greater transactional distances need more autonomy. Identifying the critical elements in the various forms of teaching and learning in a ODL environment.

The open systems approach can provide the fundamental context for the critical study of ODL because of its potential value in "synthesising and analysing complexity". This complexity includes:

i) A large number of activities to be integrated including course design and development, production, delivery, teaching and student support;
ii) A variety of specialist personnel and resource inputs;
iii) Large numbers of students;
iv) New communication technologies;
v) Visible and relatively permanent course materials;
vi) Significant extra-institutional goals;

vii) Significant financial investments; and
viii) Significant risk.

These characteristics imply a need for coordinated management and control and integration of resources—human, physical and monetary. In complex situations, marked by the need to be flexible and adaptive, as well as an emphasis on service to clients, cost reduction, and rapid response to changing technologies, a systems approach can help assist in planning, directing, evaluating and redirecting programmes and processes.

An open system is a distinct entity that takes in resources from its environment, processes them in some way, and produces output. The components of the open system are relationally arranged and interdependent "in order to attain its specified purpose". A systems approach looks both inward and outward, focusing on relationships and patterns of interaction between subsystems and their environments within the organisation.

ODL may be conceptualised and analysed from a systems perspective because it is made up a complex set of interdependent subsystems. External to a ODL programme are local, state, national, and international structures that impact on offerings and delivery systems. Within the institution, there are three major subsystems:

i) an operational system,
ii) a logistical system and
iii) a regulatory system.

The distance learning programme takes in resources and information and processes them within these subsystems in a variety of ways, returning a range of educational services and programmes to individuals and systems in its environment. The ODL programme is highly dependent on resources in the environment for its success. There are numerous examples of systems thinking in ODL.

Options identified for the management and administration of the distance learning system include: assessment methods, resource allocation, and policy development. To conceptualise a distance learning system in terms of its environment is to emphasise the importance of exchange between the distance learning programme and its environment.

Unfortunately, the forces that drive this exchange are not always the needs of the learners, but may be swayed by everything in the environment from government policies to university traditions. For example, ODL systems respond to financial imperatives in their environment in one basic way: by collecting tuition. These programmes also depend heavily on their environment's human resources to sustain a pool of qualified instructors.

Another vital form of input for distance learning systems is information, for example, knowledge of subject-specific and job-specific educational needs in a given community. The most obvious output of a distance learning programme is course content delivery, either synchronous or asynchronous. Another output may be supplemental educational resources distributed in various forms, which can be utilised over a longer period of time.

The effectiveness of this kind of output is difficult, but not impossible to measure, and may help to determine how well a distance learning programme is functioning as a system. All distance learning systems have boundaries that define what is inside and what is outside the system. Sometimes the boundaries are imprecise and fuzzy. Fundamental to this imprecision is the idea that there is no one best way to organise. Just as with living organisms, the effectiveness of a ODL organisation depends on the alignment among characteristics of the system and between the system and its environment.

ODL is also suitable for those who for social, economic or educational reasons missed out on the opportunities available from traditional institutions offered at traditional times and places, or who wish to retrain or update themselves, or study for personal interest and enjoyment. A whole range of enrichment, community development and vocational education distance courses are possible for adults, including distance learning opportunities provided by firms for the delivery of training opportunities on the job.

Improvements in one part of the distance learning environment must be accompanied by improvements in related areas and all must be monitored carefully so that gains in one part of the ODL organisation will not lead to the loss of benefits somewhere else. When viewed in terms of transformation processes, a distance learning system may be viewed as an entity designed to incorporate input from the environment, transform the input into output, distribute that output into the environment, and make adjustments as necessary to the changing conditions of the environment.

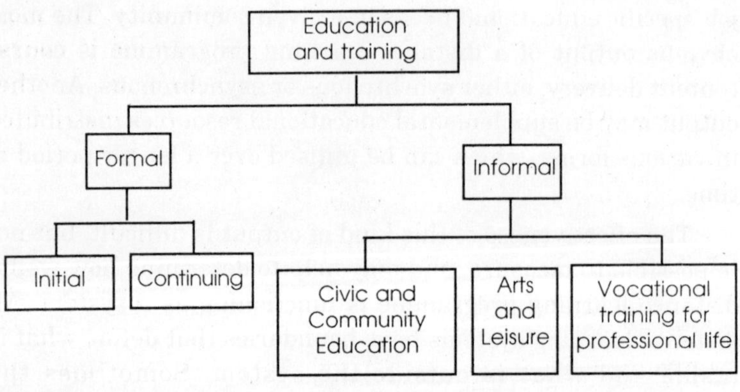

Figure 4.1: Different types of ODL situations

ODL is becoming a rapidly expanding group of offerings and activities. Lifelong learning, educational flexibility and growth in student populations are among the trends feeding this expansion. However, the ODL audience is not homogeneous. "The intended audience for distributed learning can be segmented into numerous categories, ranging from traditional students seeking additional flexibility to 'recreational learners' engaged in expanding their personal knowledge." A number of different characteristics can help define a learner segment:

i) Age/maturity
ii) Motivation (e.g., earn a degree vs. recreational learning)
iii) Type of credential desired (e.g., degree, certificate) campus)

The diversity of new organisational models supporting ODL development and delivery is noteworthy. These models now include new stand-alone degree programmes offered by online institutions, degree programmes granted by online consortia; non-degree opportunities offered by online consortia; educational opportunities offered by corporate universities; and online programmes and courses offered by organisations that are not affiliated with institutions and that may or may not include degrees or other credentials.

For-profit ODL programmes are highly competitive because they pay close attention to service levels for learners, efficiently use staff to serve students, mandate teacher training, enforce rigorous evaluation of the teaching process, emphasise supporting all teachers, including part timers, and focus on professional expertise. The tools and methods that play a crucial role in the educational programmes provided by commercial ODL providers include:

i) Collaborative environment tools allowing students to connect with instructors anywhere.
ii) Multimedia learning materials prepared by a few experts and used by many more.
iii) Use of network technologies allowing student to learn anywhere, anytime.

Learning management systems which facilitate the monitoring of the user's progress, the diagnosis of the learner's needs and problems and the adjustment of structure and flow of content and of instructional system to effectively address learning objectives and needs. The world of for-profit education is further complicated by the fact that many of the best known non-profit universities, both public and private, have established for-profit subsidiaries or joined with for-profit firms in joint educational enterprises.

Distance learning has the ability to move far beyond these characteristics in serving new learners, by eliminating geographic barriers, providing instruction at the convenience of the student, and transforming ideas about student-faculty relationships, faculty load, and institutional autonomy. Academic distance learning programmes suffer from a dearth of standards and recognised leaders in the field, and an abundance of unproved technologies. Complexities surrounding the adoption of ODL technologies are compounded by the continued inability to resolve issues within the larger learning environment. Many contend that higher education institutions cannot respond quickly enough either to the needs of learners or to the solving of policy issues that are evolving out of new educational delivery models. Transforming higher education systems through the mainstreaming of distance learning into the academic infrastructure will affect all educational management systems.

Distance learning, with its demand for different infrastructure and support systems, demands new ways of operating, new support structures for faculty and staff and new funding formulas. Distance learning, with its capacity for flexibility and just-in-time learning, challenges assumptions about the academic calendar, space planning, and scheduling that are as old as the Academy itself.

Distance learning efforts are found marginalised in continuing education programmes and divisions. Consequently: their influence on core programmes, operating assumptions and values remain low. Their capacity for adapting to changing markets is often resented rather than appreciated by campus-based faculty, staff, and students, who see such efforts as diverting precious resources, offering lower quality education, threatening time-honoured conceptions of teaching and learning, and diminishing the status of institutions.

The major barrier is the lack of computer or online service both in the home and in school. The capacity of information and communication technology has been growing exponentially over the last 10 to 15 years. Computers are now more powerful, satellite and wireless technology has increased transmission capacity, the cost of bandwidth is falling, the reach of digital satellite transponders and fibre optic cable for broad bandwidth are increasing, "last mile" solutions are becoming more prevalent, and software development such as multimedia authoring systems are making it easier to create digital materials such as computer simulations and education materials. Despite the increased capacity of information and communication technologies, the impact in higher education has been slow and marginal. This is due not only to lack of vision or commitment by educators and policy makers; there are significant structural and cultural barriers or restrictions that have slowed the potential for change in education compared with other sectors.

ASESSMENT OF TECHNOLOGY USE

No one technology can support all types of teaching and learning at a distance—the most effective approach is to combine a range of technologies. Using multiple types of media (video, audio, and data) ensures that "all learning styles are met and that significant methods for interaction are provided." Each of these media serves a specific purpose:

i) A strong print component can provide much of the basic instructional content in the form of a course text, as well as readings, the syllabus, and day-to-day schedule.

ii) Interactive audio or videoconferencing can provide real time face-to-face (or voice-to-voice) interaction. This is also an excellent and cost-effective way to incorporate guest speakers and content experts.

iii) Computer conferencing or electronic mail can be used to send messages, assignment feedback, and other targeted communication to one or more class members. It can also be used to increase interaction among students.

iv) Pre-recorded video (on tape or CD/DVD) can be used to present class lectures and visually-oriented content.

v) Fax can be used to distribute assignments, last-minute announcements, to receive student assignments and to provide timely feedback.

vi) The widespread use of wireless personal digital assistants (PDA) and embedded screens in cellular phones is now providing both enhanced communication and interaction.

The increase in the power of personal computers is leading the way toward virtual reality learning environments. Technologies such as head mounted displays and data gloves are providing interfaces for immersive, partially immersive and enhanced reality environments.

Online technology designed to mimic the classroom becomes a restriction and a barrier to the teacher's ability to impart knowledge. A fundamental paradigm shift is necessary to create a pedagogical model with the asynchronous technological interface in mind. The pedagogy must allow for flexibility, interactivity, and media-rich and adaptive environments that both provide individualised learning and are also accessible to large numbers of learners for collaborations and group discussions.

There is strong consensus in the research community that technology and technology-enhanced programmes can support engaged learning at a distance. Researchers have identified many features of technology that are important to learning high-technology performance, organised within seven categories:

i) Access to appropriate and diverse technologies and resources, both on campus and beyond campus;
ii) Operability of the technology;
iii) Organisation of the technology, in terms of its location and distribution;
iv) "Engagability", or the capacity of the technology to help students be engaged with learning;
v) Ease of use;
vi) Functionality or the technology's capacity to serve learning needs; and
vii) Reliability of the technology is as "failsafe" as possible.

Campuses need to carefully consider whether they are well positioned to provide the requisite technological infrastructure to support ODL courses and programmes. The role of consortia and other alliances is growing in order to leverage the content provided by specialists in given fields. Most universities have a strategy for promoting their ODL initiatives. Most also have an overall strategic plan for the institution in general. However, very few bring the two together and have a central policy for the use of technology both at a distance and on campus that is part of the overall university strategic plan.

The new ODL force transforming higher education may not be controlled by the traditional structures or providers of education or by traditional academic policies. Technology offers the possibility of "unbundling"—taking apart—various educational functions and roles within academic institutions. For example, distance learning encourages the unbundling of different instructional elements:

i) content development,
ii) course delivery,
iii) testing and evaluation,
iv) administrative functions—registration, payment and student record keeping.

Table 4.1
Distance Learning Technologies: Strengths and Limitations

	Strengths	*Limitations*
Traditional Face-to-face meetings, workshops, and classes	Can use all senses; may be easier to receive immediate feedback; people most accustomed to face-to-face meetings; may be rewards associated with travel.	Can involve considerable costs if people need to travel to learning site; participation may be limited due to time or distance conflicts.
Work station-time shifting VCR, computer, CD-ROM, DVD	Good for delivery of material at variable times.	Production costs can be high; location specific.
Real-time distance learning (Two-way video and two-way audio)	Two-way video and two-way audio- can see and hear; opportunity for immediate feedback; students may not need to travel to participate in learning; medium-range variable costs, but international connection costs may be considerable.	Compressed video will allow the ability to see limited number of sites at the same time; some video distortion due to compression of signal; high fixed costs, reliability of equipment, may be questionable; no opportunity for time shifting unless combined with another technology.
Satellite (one-way video and two-way audio)	Good for reaching large area that is geographically dispersed and/or large number of downlink sites; high variable costs; participants may not need to travel to participate in learning activities	Two-way audio, but only one way video. Originating site can't see remote sites; high fixed costs for uplink site; requires considerable coordination, technical support; no opportunity for time shifting unless combined with another technology.

Synchronous, computer	Relatively low fixed costs and low telecommunications costs; opportunity for immediate feedback.	Can be chaotic and confusing; primarily text based and graphic communication; users must have access to computer and modem; no opportunity for time shifting.
Audioconferencing	Wide access to telephones; relatively low variable costs and low fixed costs; can be time shifting; opportunity for immediate feedback; highly interactive.	Audio only; no opportunity for time shifting
Asynchronous distance learning Video-based courses	Video-cassette players widely available; offers sight, sound and motion; opportunity for re-play; opportunity for timeshifting; almost unlimited in terms of what can be sent.	One-way communication; may encounter high "drop out" rate; production costs may be high; international formats may be incompatible.
Computers and modems	Production costs are variable, depending on the message transmission; opportunity for timeshifting; highly interactive; permits just-in-time access to information.	Primarily text-based and graphics; message can appear "flat".
Multimedia on demand (just in time)	Accessible from user's location; no limit to what can be sent, but mostly print-based; opportunity for timeshifting	Production costs can be very high Requires high bandwidth
Correspondence courses		Not very popular anymore; requires self-motivated learning who are good time managers; interactivity is slow and difficult

ODL ENVIRONMENT: ASSESSMENT OF STANDARDS

Many of the important trends and issues in the ODL world today relate to the concepts of unbundling and standardising of higher education processes for use in the ODL environment. Some of the trends influencing the "unbundling" process are:

i) The evolution of "standards based learning systems" that allow content to be defined in small objects with associated learning resources, activities and assessment strategies which can then be shared among institutions that adhere to similar technical standards.
ii) Associated with the above is the development of content standards as a means of quality assurance.
iii) The evolution of new organisations that specialise in providing key functions such as development of instructional materials, and provision of technical delivery systems, learning assessment and learner support services.

Perhaps of greatest significance currently in the distance learning environment is the emergence of what is being referred to as the development of standards-based learning objects. The vision "involves the organisation of content into small objects in the form of learning outcomes and associating them with learning resources, activities and assessment strategies." These objects can then be tagged and managed in a learning object repository and assembled into learning modules or courses as needed.

Learning objects can be thought of as learning content that is as granular as a 'text tip' or as involved as an 'interactive Java applet' lesson. The concept of 'granular' learning objects is the driving concept behind some online learning environments. Through the process of creating these learning objects, a method for preparing digital learning resources and courses for use, reuse, re-purposing and electronic commerce is created.

The structure of the educational materials is linked with a standard classification system that facilitates the storage and retrieval of the content by any institution that uses the same standards. The development of a learning resource classification scheme is leading to the use of open specifications and a basic vocabulary for describing learning resources called metadata. Metadata is simply a formatted file containing text that provides descriptive information about content. This information may include the format, size, delivery requirements, authorship, ownership, version number, instructional role, instructional characteristics, and type of interactivity.

Items retrieved through the use of metadata can be re-aggregated according to the needs of a group of learners, and the material can be reproduced in print, CD-ROM, or web-based delivery formats as appropriate. The purpose of Advanced Distributed Learning (ADL) is to exploit existing network-based technologies; create platform neutral, reusable courseware and content to lower costs; promote widespread collaboration to satisfy common needs; enhance performance with emerging and next generation learning technologies; develop a common framework that drives the commercial off-the-shelf cycle; establish a coordinated implementation process; and develop common standards and guidelines.

The development of standards-based learning systems is leading to the need to produce content standards as well. Content is essentially the material used to convey the subject matter. It may include text, graphics, audio, some form of interaction and concept application. The development of learning resources for the ODL environment is particularly expensive, with costs running three to 10 times those of traditional courses. A major challenge in considering content exchange is in evaluating the quality of the content available on the web, by considering its contextual accuracy, pedagogical soundness and ease of use.

MERLOT (Multimedia Educational Resource for Learning and Online Teaching) is a project that addresses these challenges through a cooperatively developed, free, web-based resource that faculty can access to find digital learning materials with evaluations and guidance for use.

Higher education software can be broken into two segments: applications that automate administrative services and applications that enable pieces of the learning process. The learning content management market is much more fragmented, with commercially companies like Web CT and Blackboard competing with "do it yourself applications" and shareware. Typically, these tools enable professors to post course information on the web, link to educational resources, provide chat room capability and discussion board applications and the like.

The potential value of learning content management technologies increases as they are combined with administrative systems enterprise applications to provide a complete DL environment. There are three main obstacles for providing effective enterprise level e-learning environments. These are:

i) Lack of support for the collaborative and dynamic nature of learning.
ii) Lack of standards for locating and operating interactive platform-independent materials.
iii) Lack of incentives and structure for developing and sharing content.

Development tools are built into the course management system environment, enabling instructors to create web pages, upload documents, design online quizzes and tests, and add such features as email, threaded discussion, and chat. Course management tools support collaborative online activities that are comparable in interactivity to that available in traditional face-to-face classrooms as well as a standard interface for developing and distributing course content.

One of the challenges facing universities and colleges is to decide which pieces and parts to buy, build or partner to acquire and which components to use in their ODL environment. In 1998, the Western Cooperation for Educational Telecommunications (WCET) conducted a survey of student services for distance learning. The WCET report covered more than 400 institutions representing the 15 state western regions. At that time, online programmes were in an "early adoption" state, and a majority had not adapted student services for an online environment.

The distance learning enterprise grows, important questions continue to be raised about the ability of colleges and universities to provide socialisation opportunities for students at a distance. The kinds of student services that have expanded on many campuses, including activities that, for example, encourage appreciation of diversity or provide leadership experiences, are now considered to be significant in the ODL environment as well.

The current trend for ODL students is towards an integrated portal system, which supports teaching, learning, administration and management and provides:

i) A web interface with courseware and required information about courses
ii) Online access to grades, financial aid information, class schedules and graduation checks
iii) Access to the communities of interest within the university
iv) Increased lifelong learning opportunities

The web is used as a flexible and highly functional medium for promoting interaction between students and faculty and other professional staff and with each other. Virtual office hours, shared work spaces, internet discussion groups and forums are being created to provide environments for interaction. Particularly in the distance environment, the importance of students' support for each other "to keep them going" cannot be underestimated.

As ODL proliferates in response to increases in demand as well as to an increase in the number and variety of organisations offering ODL opportunities. The key stakeholders in the ODL environment include students, the institution itself, faculty, student services personnel, and external oversight bodies such as the government, funding agencies, and accreditation bodies. Any ODL system incorporates many different elements and processes and the actual degree of importance given to these varying components depends upon which interest group is going to interpret quality.

The most common form of evaluation of ODL courses and teaching relies rather heavily on student questionnaires, even though some study suggests that the instruments used "are not geared to evaluation of online teaching and learning".

The challenge in using traditional accreditation processes in a ODL environment is that traditional assessment standards have literally required that higher education take place in a physical form. With distance learning, education is not a place, but a process. The challenge faced by those in the ODL environment to validate their learning, though difficult, is not impossible.

As online pedagogy develops, it is replacing tests with portfolios, individual grades with group projects, and single assignments with iterative projects that require revision and re-thinking. When ODL finishes implementing outcome measures of learning for its programmes, the rest of higher education will have no choice but to follow suit.

The motivation for establishing methodologies for assessing the cost of distance learning is fuelled by the desire to reach more learners while at the same time responding to the pressure to reduce costs, increase efficiency, and maintain high quality. There are now many references in the literature to the potential for cost savings and return on investment as one of the benefits of distance learning. In theory, reducing costs as distance learning opportunities expand may be possible.

A 1996 study prepared for the European Association of Distance Teaching Universities showed that "creating a distance-learning programme involves so many variables—from programme type and size to the source and cost of course materials that building revenues while cutting expenses is merely a possibility, not a certainty." The fact that conclusive reliable results of cost-benefit studies are not being found suggests that no one yet has succeeded.

Cost-effectiveness "is a mode of cost-aware institutional operation, which takes into account quality and benefits to all stakeholders, and allows comparisons with similar institutions to be drawn". ODL is beneficial when effectiveness is measured by achievement, by attitudes of students and teachers, and by cost-effectiveness.

For the majority of educational institutions, i.e., those whose missions are not specifically dedicated to distance learning, the emergence of asynchronous methods of course delivery presents these institutions with major challenges related to both technological and organisational change. Strategies for institutional decision making related to the ODL concept are being developed to help "steer" institutions "through the rapids" of transformation.

Many colleges and universities have already launched major strategic efforts to understand, be responsive to and be transformed by their response to ODL issues. Such efforts to explore new models of learning extend far beyond the traditional higher education enterprise to include an array of new participants, including publishing houses, entertainment companies, information services provides, and information technology corporations.

It is clear that access to advanced learning opportunities is not only becoming a more pervasive need, but could well become a defining domestic policy issue for a knowledge-driven society. Some institutions are continuing to develop and support their own distributed learning environments. Although economics and politics were early drivers, peer pressure and changing customer expectations have become increasingly important motivators in this regard. The cost and complexity of individually-developed and maintained ODL structures "will almost certainly serve as a significant barrier to individualised solutions" to ODL programme development and delivery in the future.

REFERENCES

Belanger, F. and D.H. Jordan, *Evaluation and Implementation of Distance Learning: Technologies, Tools, and Techniques*, Hershey, Pa.: Idea Group Publishing, 2000.

Bates, Tony, "The Continuing Evolution of ICT Capacity: The Implications for Education" In Farrell, Glen, (ed.), *The Changing Face of Virtual Education*. London: The Commonwealth of Learning, 2001, p. 29- 46.

Bonamy, J., B. Charlier, and M., Saunders, 'Bridging Tools' for change: evaluating a collaborative learning network. *Journal of Computer Assisted Learning,* Vol. 17 (3) 295-305, 2001.

Capper, Joanne, "E-Learning Growth and Promise for the Developing World", *TechKnowLogia*, May/June, 2001, p. 7-10.

Cooper, Mark N., *Disconnected, Disadvantaged, and Disenfranchised: Explorations in the Digital Divide*, Washington, D.C.: Consumer Federation of American and Consumers Union, 2000.

Floor P., Networked Services for Quality Distance Learning, in *ODL Networking for Quality Learning,* in Proceedings of Lisbon 2000 Conference of the European ODL Liaison Committee, Lisbon, 2000.

Perraton, H. (ed.), *Distance Education: An Economic and Educational Assessment of its Potential,* World Bank. 1986.

_______________ and C., Creed, *Applying new technologies and cost-effective delivery systems in basic education*, Paris: UNESCO, 2000 .

Nisbet, J., "Issues/Questions", In *Curricular Reform: Assessment in Question*, Paris, OECD, 1993.

Rowntree, D., *Exploring Open and Distance Learning*, London: Kogan Page, 1992.

Tait, A., *Quality Assurance in Distance Education: International Case Studies*, Vancouver: The Commonwealth of Learning, 1997.

5

Global Challenges

With the advent of ICTs, educational institutions around the world are looking at what these new technologies and open and distance learning (ODL) offers both for their existing students and for potential new students. It is also seen as an important means for facilitating cooperation and collaboration between different educational actors and institutions within and across the globe. Much of the political interest in lifelong learning is of course a reaction and response to the so-called transition from the industrialised society to the information society.

The increased capacity for global communication, together with the easy access to information-rich repositories accessible via the internet and/or world wide web has led educationalist to suggest we need to change our teaching and learning approaches. The traditional role of university and college lecturers has been until now one of expert researcher and/or teacher in their declared field of study. In the role of teacher they have traditionally been required to convey to their students a critical understanding of the accepted body of knowledge in our field. However, on the one hand the very idea that there is an accepted single body of knowledge in a given field has itself been seriously challenged from a number of different stances, in recent years. And, on the other hand, the increase in access to ideas and knowledge, some would argue, is or will inevitably radically change these expectations upon the role of teachers.

In this information age it is not the amount of information teachers hold in their heads which are important but the way they use and create information that is in their computers and accessible through the WWW. There is however a more widespread acceptance of the need to be considering the use of less instructional approaches and move towards more constructional approaches to teaching and learning.

ICT-supported ODL with both its capacity to increase access to information and, it must be said, to provide support for communication and collaboration between learners is seen by many as potentially more inherently able to support constructionist approaches to teaching and learning. Let us not forget that technology cannot in itself determine educational practice. Indeed, if we look at what actually happens in the great majority of existing web-based and online courses there remains a large instructional dimension to them.

There is still a wide difference between theory and practice with respect to interest in constructionist approaches to learning. The eight indices of constuctionism are:

i) ethos/environment (learner-centred; tutor or content centred; neutral or indecisive
ii) authenticity of content (realistic/real world; theoretical)
iii) learners' personal experiences (sought or offered and utilised; not sought or utilised)
iv) learner-learner interaction (encouraged; not sought; encouraged and tutor participation)
v) learner "thinking aloud" (development of student own line of thinking encouraged; not sought or encouraged)
vi) feedback on contributions (positive and encouraged; negative or dismissive)
vii) development of thinking skills/understanding (dominant; partial or incident neglected)
viii) learners contributions to tutorials (publicly valued; not valued; not sought)

Ignorance of constructionism is likely to be the main explanation of the inability or reluctance of tutors to conduct what were labelled tele-tutorials but were in it seems in practice largely monological mini-lectures. Within the constraints of existing educational and indeed accreditation systems it is not an easy thing to move from predominately instructional-based approaches to teaching and learning to more constructionist ones.

Recent surveys of ODL projects reveal that they had explicitly struggled with the issues involved a key aspect of all of their experiences was the significance and importance of confronting states of uncertainty when working with more constructionist models of teaching and learning. The need to come to terms with and accept complexity and diversity when and if working across the kind of boundaries and constraints they encountered was perhaps the key idea/issue to emerge from examination of the projects.

What is perhaps most interesting about the ODL projects is that they all by definition have to work with complex situations and differences. This is the case whether or not they are in practice either attempting to work with constructionist principles of education or even really engage with the different educational challenges and/or opportunities that arise from being able to offer courses via the web or via other online environments. By definition they have to have partners from at least three different countries and this immediately brings up cultural and language differences, different education traditions and different perspectives on issues and indeed on the status and nature of knowledge. They are as one might expect more or less successful in dealing with these differences.

Some of the issues or problems that the projects most frequently mention are;

i) Use of the English language as the linguafranco

ii) Insufficient acknowledgment of different approaches and attitudes to

iii) UG/Master/Doctoral work in different countries

iv) Difficulties of integration and academic recognition of work done online as opposed to as part of conventional studies/courses

v) Difficulties of coordinating the timing of virtual meetings

vi) Insufficient attention given to the process and the changing or different roles/responsibilities of both tutors and students.

A Belgium-coordinated project named Learn-net is a higher education project that aims to develop a collaborative learning environment for teacher education students from nine institutions in five different countries. The intention was to provide the pedagogical support and tools for students to do collaborative projects with students from another university than their own. What is interesting about Learn-nett is its recognition of the need to both provide a central frame and allow for local autonomy. They sought to attain a common vision of collaborative learning shared by all partners without imposing a common solution for implementing that vision. In practice this meant that each university designed its own pedagogical scenario within which the collaborative projects were located taking into account both they are own situation and the common characteristics of the learning environment.

Some aspects were consequently constant across the institutions and some variable. They are:

i) The subject domains should be wide with low specifications of content.

ii) The learning environment should have high specification of learning process the learning environment should allow for high level of learner decision making on content.

iii) Subject tutors should adopt the role of facilitator, not instructor.

iv) Learning process takes place in team.

v) A technical infrastructure must be in place.

vi) A minimum of technical and procedural training must be offered.

vii) Additional time is required for group formation, decisions on project goals, methods, etc.

viii) Different time allocation and assessment requirements of members of the cross institutional team should be specified.

ix) Tutors will help teams to develop flexible academic outcomes so that aspects of collaborative experience can be assessed at different times in the learning process.

x) The collaboration should allow for different exit points.

New technology and associated ODL courses allow greater co-operation and collaboration at global level. It has been claimed that the big players will come to dominate the education market and become global providers. Institutions working in partnership with large corporate organisations are the biggest threat to existing institutions and approaches to higher education.

Today, there is an enormous increase in the number of corporate universities globally. From this trend it can be assumed that education is being transformed into the learning business and there are many new and highly influential players on the global scene. It is not just the corporate universities, it is the for-profit businesses as well. It will be the profit-making business firms rather than the non-profit universities that will be the best positioned to be the prime educational institutions of the future.

ODL IN DEVELOPING WORLD: MEEITNG THE CHANGING DEMANDS

Education is always related to the economic, social and cultural development of the society. The importance of knowledge as an essential component of the economy has influenced the increasing interest of governments in human knowledge resource development. The tendency has been evident in developing as well as developed countries, although the circumstances, priorities and challenges are different. The resources available for the development of knowledge are far from evenly distributed. In spite of a considerable quantitative growth in recent years, there are still intolerable inequalities both between and within nations. There are about 880 million illiterate adults in the world and some 113 million children between six and 11 deprived of any schooling at all. Besides the insufficiency of opportunity, the low quality of education and its frequently observed irrelevance are also of major concern. Rapid changes in the workforce, unemployment and uncertainty now demand fast-changing, just in time, continuing and lifelong education.

Lack of resources in developing countries is obvious, and becomes more acute as demographic trends increase the need to expand educational provision. A developing country has to find new methods that will dramatically improve both its children's schooling and its continuing education system. New methods will need new organisational forms, which in turn require rethinking of education and training policies. Strategies that have been recommended include the diversification of the resource base by privatising some educational functions, the use of donations from private sources, and the recovery of costs from users and participants. Another strategy is to focus on increasing efficiency within the system. The future policy will probably involve structural reform and the limitation of expenditure in the public sector. It is therefore relevant to look not only at new technologies but also alternative systemic approaches in pursuit of increasing access, improving cost-effectiveness and quality, as well as learning outcomes.

Development of a more knowledge-based and service-oriented economy leads to important changes in the organisation of work and the structure of skills needed. New jobs tend to demand new and higher levels of skills, customer-oriented communication, problem solving and entrepreneurial skills. The emergence of more flexible work organisations is clearly linked to the development of technology. One of the new challenges for education is high-level skills that are needed.

Increasing integration and interdependence of national economies are followed by attempts towards economic integration at regional levels. International and regional cooperation in education and training is often included in such efforts. Internationalisation is enhanced by the development of information and communication technologies. Thus, international and regional markets for education and training are emerging. This leads not only to increased international awareness and orientation in curricula, but also facilitates the exchange and sharing of expertise and human resources.

Increased communication underlines the needs for mutual information and understanding of cultural and social contexts. Sometimes cultural and ethnic forces oppose internationalisation, leading to an increase in national, ethnic and regional consciousness and in the extreme to polarisation and fragmentation. The challenge to education is to prepare citizens for a truly international community, without neglecting the richness and the value of cultural variation. As in every other walk of modern life, the answer to the challenge of education for development will include the use of information and communication technologies, provided the necessary organisational and policy changes can be implemented to make the technologies effective.

A range of technological devices is now widely available and relatively cheap. They are accepted and often available for domestic use as well as in the workplace. Governments are concerned that educational institutions become connected to the emerging networks, that curricula include the knowledge of and acquaintance with new technologies, and that teachers are prepared and trained to use these new resources. Among the benefits expected from new information and communication technologies, besides that of outreach, are efficiencies derived from economies of scale and qualitative improvements such as greater individualisation of learning, easier access to information, and more use of simulation techniques. In addition, the use of new forms of technology will have an impact on the cognitive functions of children and youth.

In efforts to meet the new and changing demands for education and training, open and distance learning may be seen as an approach that is at least complementary and under certain circumstances an appropriate substitute for the face-to-face methods that still dominate most educational systems. While its benefits can be evaluated by technical, social and economic criteria, distance learning methods also have their own pedagogical merit, leading to different ways of conceiving knowledge generation and acquisition. To the learner, open and distance learning means more freedom of access, and thereby a wider range of opportunities for learning and qualification.

The barriers that may be overcome by distance learning include not only geographical distance, but also other confining circumstances, such as personal constraints, cultural and social barriers and lack of educational infrastructure. For the student it is often a cheaper alternative to pursuing a course through conventional methods. Since many people cannot afford to leave their work in order to study, it is important that distance education and training may be combined with work. Distance and open learning may also mean a more learner-centred approach, allowing greater flexibility and choice of content as well as more personal organisation of the learning programme. For employers, open and distance learning offers the possibility of organising learning and professional development in the workplace itself, which is often more flexible and saves costs of travel, subsistence etc.

The use of distance learning often puts both the firm and employees in a position of co-investment in the pursuit of common goals, based on shared values and culture. It increases productivity and supports the development of communication and other work-related skills. With sufficient numbers of employees being trained, open and distance learning is usually cost-effective. Other advantages for the employer include the increased availability of the employee during the course of the training programme, and the portability of training programmes and processes. These advantages to learners and employers are also important features from the perspective of governments.

Traditionally, governments have introduced distance education provision in order to:

i) increase access to learning and training opportunity; provide increased opportunities for updating, retraining and personal enrichment;
ii) improve cost-effectiveness of educational resources; support the quality and variety of existing educational structures;
iii) enhance and consolidate capacity.

In the light of the experiences of the past 20 or more years, there is today recognition of other, related, benefits. Some of these are:

i) balancing inequalities between age groups;
ii) extending geographical access to education;
iii) delivering educational campaigns and other education for large audiences;
iv) providing speedy and efficient training for key target groups;
v) expanding the capacity for education in new and multi-disciplinary subject areas;
vi) offering the combination of education with work and family life;
vii) developing multiple competencies through recurrent and continuing education;

viii) enhancing the international dimension of educational experience;

ix) improving the quality of existing educational services.

Today, open and distance learning has become one of the most rapidly growing fields of education and training. It is fast becoming an accepted and indispensable part of the mainstream of educational systems in both developed and developing countries, with particular importance for the latter. This growth has been stimulated in part by interest among educators and trainers in the use of new, internet-based information technologies, but also by recognition that traditional ways of organising education need to be reinforced by innovative methods if the fundamental right of all people to a life of learning is to be realised. Governments around the world are becoming more aware of the potential of open and distance learning and it is essential for their educational planning that the opportunities offered be realistically examined within the framework of national development plans in general and educational policies in particular.

REFERENCES

Dodd, T. and J. K. Mayo, "The Promise and Performance of Distance Education in Developing Nations: The IEC experience 1971-1992", Paper presented at International Extension College's Anniversary Conference, Robinson College Cambridge UK, September 1992.

Lockwood, F. (ed.), *Open and Distance Learning Today*, London, Routledge.

Perraton, H., *Open and Distance Learning in the Developing World*, London, Routledge, 2000.

Sherry, L S. "Issues in Distance Learning", *International Journal of Distance Education*, vol.1, 1996.

Wurster, S., *Distance Education: Beneath the Surface*, Techtrends, 1996.

6

Internet and Web-based Strategy

Over the past few decades, the development of a range of technologies has accelerated exponentially, mainly due to the invention of digital electronics. A vital recent development has been the convergence of technology concerned mainly with the processing of information with that which deals mainly with its communication. This is clearly seen in the emergence of the internet, whereby the processing power in each office and school can easily be connected, and can communicate with corresponding systems anywhere else in the world.

The use of the internet in the sphere of organisation and management of education leads to the increase of education accessibility on a global scale, and may lead to the growth of economic efficiency of an educational institution's activity. All developed countries of the world have more or less extensive programmes of internet development in the sphere of education. The overwhelming majority of developing countries, despite difficulties, problems and fears, seek as far as possible to take part in the formation of the global educational community.

The creation of mechanisms designed for effective navigation of the internet, and the collection, analysis, exchange and distribution of information for the specific use of education acquires great importance. However, despite the outstanding progress made in some countries in the creation of universal information retrieval systems and specialised information systems for education, neither set of systems taken separately can provide a complete service.

Application of the internet in education is understood as the use of various internet-technologies for the solution of various educational tasks, namely, teaching, learning and management of the educational process. It has usually been found that only two or three out of the 20 current internet-applications are used in most educational institutions. Further, this situation arises from a lack of information rather than a lack of finance. A powerful tool for the solution of the resultant problems can however be provided on the basis of the co-operation between such systems. The specialised information system 'Education via the Internet' within the framework of UNESCO programme activity may become one of a group of permanent international tools of cooperation.

The world wide web offers a global forum to teach courses. Each student at any time has an excellent encyclopedia at his or her disposal. Course material can be dynamically updated. Course text, examples and exercises can be interactive in the sense of immediately illustrating equations with graphs, changing parameters and seeing the results, linking to other websites according to the interests of the student. Web-based learning model is essentially free from limitations of space and time while it reaches students around the world with great ease. In addition, the model offers students a wealth of information that was never possible in the classical model.

The possibility of linking to information worldwide in a multitude of formats creates a remarkably rich medium for learning. Web-based courseware is not merely an electronic duplicate of the original course material. It represents a new type of educational materials which takes full advantage of the emerging web and multimedia technologies in order to achieve an effective yet enjoyable learning process. Thus, complex concepts are introduced in innovative ways. Full linking to vast resources available worldwide introduces new levels of value to the courseware.

A web-based course is developed through the efforts of a team of professionals with a complementary range of skills, as opposed to classical course design, which is typically developed by faculty alone. The richness of modern web and multimedia technologies allow for unlimited creativity when it comes to electronic courseware development. Such richness offers educators new opportunities to develop very interesting course material while it also poses a substantial challenge in that it requires faculty to rethink their own course offerings in the light of the new technologies. Today technology is creating a new educational platform and is reconfiguring the way a student learns. Networked learning—accessing libraries, scholars, networks, and information worldwide—is evolving.

Education is a discovery process, and its mission is to provide the widest repertoire of possibilities for a student entering a learning situation. Technology can realise this ambition, and because of it a student's educational experience can be immeasurably richer. Various typologies of Internet Applications in Education (IAE) have been proposed in the literature in recent years. Two main approaches to the segmentation of this project-domain have been revealed through the analysis of recent experience. The technology-oriented approach is the most widespread. For example, statistical research on the use of the electronic communication in open and distance learning, conducted by UNESCO in 1995, has identified the following types of applied telecommunication media in educational programmes: telephone; fax; audio-conference; videoconference; electronic mail; access to databases.

For a long time electronic mail has remained the only internet application in education. Still e-mail continue as the most frequently used computer technology in open and distance learning. A relatively new phenomenon in educational communications is the newly established practice of learners speaking directly to experts in one or another field (which can already be considered as a consequence of the increase in the level of communication skills among learners actively using the Internet). On the net, there are a number of centres such as Yahoo! Yahooligans! School Bell; Homework Answers; and Ask a Scientist. By addressing enquiries to these centres learners can receive, via e-mail, answers to their questions on a particular theme.

An online lecture or presentation of teaching material published on the net becomes accessible to many learners. At the first stage of IAE implementation, the most common technology for this communications paradigm was the electronic bulletin board (BBS) and electronic mail discussion lists (list-servs), where course notes were given with read-only access for students. Since the extensive implementation of interactive WWW technologies in the distribution of educational information, various forms of courses on the WWW have become common. WWW technologies have made it possible for materials on the net to be published with ease.

As is well known, the WWW was created as an environment specifically designed for collaborative work on documents by groups of researchers remote from each other. The further development of internet technologies has provided the opportunity for joint use and the editing of textual materials, and also of audio- and video-sequences. Problems of legislative and public control over internet contents are a part of a general problem, which can be identified as the transcultural nature of the net. It can offer a considerable challenge for the cultural identity of the nations of the world.

New technologies pose in particular questions of their influence on the culture. In some countries, governments have a negative view of internet access since it can break the culture. The limited capacity of data delivery channels creates technical restrictions for enquiries to data and knowledge bases, especially those of a multimedia nature.

Application of internet-technologies to educational systems at different levels has a significant impact on the development of open and distance learning-related forms of teaching. Traditional methods of delivery of educational materials and organisation of feedback to learners —such as mail and telephone — are increasingly being replaced by electronic mail and the WWW. Educational institutions of different types and educational levels now provide greater or lesser elements of their teaching through the WWW. An example of the use of internet-technologies in higher education is represented by those specialised distance education institutions delivering a considerable part of educational materials through the WWW. Further, many traditional higher education establishments have introduced separate distance courses.

Although open and distance learning at the current time is predominantly represented in higher education, it is gradually also beginning to be used in high schools. The areas of secondary education where this has taken place are:

a) home education: as a result of the availability of WWW resources, children suffer to a lesser extent from shortage of educational materials and a lack of dialogue with classmates —two main disadvantages of home education.
b) alternative education arising in the context of freedom of choice of school is sometimes remote from the place of residence of a pupil.
c) extra courses for pupils in conventional schools, who are in particular in preparation for entry to higher education institutions.

WEB-BASED ODL STRATEGIES

Open, flexible and distance learning strategies can benefit from the use of network technologies, connecting learners with distributed learning resources. These strategies make education more accessible, convenient and cost-effective for both the learners and the education providers. They can be used for all forms of education, extending the reach of programmes, stretching education budgets, and delivering, 'just-in-time' educational content for learners anywhere, anytime.

The challenges posed by distance teaching are countered by opportunities to reach a wider student audience:

i) to meet the needs of students who are unable to attend on-campus classes;

ii) to involve outside resources which would otherwise be unavailable;

iii) to link students from different social, cultural, economic, and experiential backgrounds.

In addition, the best courses use high quality resources such as interactive online databases, audio tapes, articles and study guides. Instructors often comment that the focused preparation required by distance teaching improves their overall teaching ability and their empathy with students. Strategies used in distance education are relevant in open and flexible education, where learning is not necessarily at a distance, i.e., enhancing campus-based learning. They have much in common; courses are usually suited to individual requirements, removing barriers that can prevent students from achieving. They are student-focused, and appropriate tutorial support is an important element of all three forms.

Common wisdom among distance educators has judged that programme development should begin by defining the purpose, audience, and content of a programme, and only then consider which technology is best suited to its delivery and use. Examples of teaching and learning with web technologies include the following:

i) Electronic mail (delivery of course materials, sending of assignments, getting and giving feedback, using a course mailing list, i.e., electronic discussion group).

ii) Bulletin boards/newsgroups for discussion of special topics.

iii) Downloading of course materials or tutorials.

iv) Interactive tutorials on the web.

v) Real-time, interactive conferencing using systems or Internet Relay Chat.

vi) "Intranets", corporate websites protected from outside access that distribute training for employees.

vii) Informatics, the use of online databases, library catalogues, and websites to acquire information and pursue research related to study.

ix) Computer Mediated Conferencing (CMC).

x) Computer Assisted Learning (CAL).

xi) Multimedia.

xii) Groupware

Asynchronous communication is communication that is not simultaneous, and uses recorded instructional materials. These types of technologies allow participants to be separated in time and distance from the delivery of instruction. Thus, telecommunications systems such as broadcast television, or electronically stored media such as video, audio, and computer software are among the technologies that utilise asynchronous communication.

Examples of other distance education technologies that are asynchronous in nature include fax machines, voice mail, bulletin boards and e-mail, computer assisted instruction, computer managed instruction, computer-mediated education and computer-based conferencing.

Synchronous communication is simultaneous. It uses technologies that facilitate live interactive instruction. Examples of synchronous communications include audio-conferencing, real-time computer communications and videoconferencing. Synchronous communication technologies, such as desktop video teleconferencing and interactive group videoteleconferencing, enable live, real-time interaction between instructors and learners.

Instructors, subject matter experts and students see and hear one another at all sites and engage in interaction, similar to face-to-face classroom interaction. Both of these forms of communication can be used in open, flexible and distance technologies. The use of desktop videoconferencing is becoming increasingly important. Desktop video systems can offer videoteleconferencing potential as well as multipoint shared software—telecollaboration. As networks reach even higher bandwidth capacity, educators will experience superior audio and video quality and multimedia capabilities that can provide many distance learning solutions. The delivery of distance education over the internet has many advantages, such as:

i) Quick development time compared to videos and CD-ROMs
ii) Easy updating and archival capabilities
iii) Lower costs compared to satellite broadcasting

For the learner, an internet course can enhance interactivity more effectively than other distance learning formats. The relative anonymity of computer communication has the potential to give voice to those reluctant to speak in face-to-face situations and to allow learners' contributions to be judged on their own merit, unaffected by iyany obvious visual cultural markersle. The medium also supports self-directed learning: computer conferencing requires learners to have motivation, self-discipline and responsibility.

At present, limited bandwidth and slow modems hamper the delivery of sound, video, and graphics, although the technology is improving all the time. Reliance on learner initiative can be a drawback for those who prefer more structure. Learner success also depends on technical skills in computer operation and internet navigation, as well as the ability to cope with technical difficulties.

Information overload is also an issue: the volume of e-mail messages to read, reflect on, and respond to, can be overwhelming. The proliferation of databases and websites demands information management skills. Access to the internet can still be a problem, especially for people with disabilities. Social isolation can be a drawback, and the lack of non-verbal cues can hinder communication.

To help learners to make effective use of distance learning methods, skilled facilitation is essential. The distance educator can employ a number of strategies focusing on planning, student understanding, interaction, and teaching to ensure a successfully delivered course. The vision which distance learning should aim towards is a seamless networked learning environment that integrates voice, video, and data connections among learners, instructors, experts, virtual libraries, the Internet, and support services.

At the centre is the learner, connected with both real-time and non-real-time links to these resources. Instructors and providers must harness the potential of synchronous and asynchronous communication technologies to create powerful, learner-centred networks. The challenge is to implement the right combination of synchronous and asynchronous technologies to create a rich mosaic of networked learning environments consistent with the mission of the educational provider, learner expectations, and the instructor's delivery style.

Resources can be used to train faculties in managing new technologies for teaching and learning at a distance, but faculties also need to adjust to a new environment—a new style of teaching and learning.

Computer Assisted Assessment (CAA) is a common term for the use of computers in the assessment of student learning. Various other forms exist, such as Computer-Aided Assessment, Computerised Assessment, and Computer-Based Assessment (CBA) . Online CBA has existed for a long time in the form of Multiple Choice Questions (MCQ's). CBA is commonly directly made via a computer, whereas CAA is used to manage or support the assessment process.

CAA is typically formative, in that it helps students to discover whether they have learned what the educator intended and provide timely feedback on how best to teach a subject. Increasingly, it can be summative, with limited feedback typically being given at the end of a course and serving to grade and categorise the student's work. It can also be diagnostic, e.g., by testing for pre-knowledge.

Assessment techniques are usually either norm referenced or criterion referenced. Norm referenced assesses an individual's performance in relation to the norms established by a peer group. Criterion referenced occurs when a student is assessed on his or her ability to meet a required level of skill or competence. CAA is usually criterion referenced.

Well-written CAA is more likely to be objective testing: it can be marked objectively and thus offer high reliability. Another benefit is that the tests can be marked quickly and easily, and adapted to meet a wide range of learning outcomes. Tests have the following potential:

i) To incorporate a wide range of media;
ii) To link online assessments to feedback;
iii) To incorporate hints into test questions;
iv) To assign other learning activities based on the test result;
v) To enable randomised selection from large question banks; and
vi) To be administrated easily, allowing better test management.

CAA can have the following limitations:

i) It is usually associated with testing low level skills rather than conceptual understanding because of the frequent use of MCQ formatting, which is believed to test at a lower level of understanding;
ii) Construction of good objective tests requires skill and practice and so is initially time consuming;
iii) Implementation of a CAA system can be costly;
iv) Hardware and software must be carefully monitored to avoid failure during examinations;

v) Security issues can be a problem in web-based CAA;

vi) Students require adequate IT skills and experience of the assessment type;

vii) Assessors and invigilators need training in assessment design, IT skills and examination management;

viii) A high level of organisation is required of all parties involved in assessment.

CAA of higher order skills such as comprehension, application and reasoning is difficult. A number of institutional CBA development projects offer free or relatively inexpensive assessment tools, which do not require the purchase of costly licences.

Widening access is a complex issue that involves differences between students' socio-economic status, gender, ability level, ethnic background, geographic location and Special Educational Needs (SEN). Network technologies are seen as a way towards developing improved resources to meet specific needs of students.

Students with learning difficulties and disabilities (SLDD) might be prevented from accessing computer opportunities because they lack adaptive devices, special software and/or information about how to adapt regular software. There are excellent sources of information to help educational managers choose assistive technology advice, software and hardware.

A computer and a modem can transport students beyond their physical environment to access electronic information. This is particularly appropriate for individuals who are distressed by going to new and busy environments such as the library. Educators with a special interest are familiar with the need to create instructional materials or customise materials to meet the varied needs of students with disabilities.

Today, there are powerful multimedia authoring and presentation tools they can use to develop and modify computer-based instructional materials for students with mild disabilities. These provide a learning tool which these students can access and use to balance their weak areas of learning with their strong areas. Authoring software allows teachers and students to develop instructional software that can incorporate video, pictures, animation, and text into hypermedia-based instruction. Multimedia authoring software is very easy to learn and use.

For the most part, adult learners are in a state of transition seeking to improve their situation through education. They cover a broad spectrum including growing numbers of women, career changers, immigrants, second career retirees, single parents, and individuals seeking professional development.

A major benefit of online learning is the ability to combine theory and practice more effectively. Active, problem-solving, goal-oriented and co-operative learning are among the more successful teaching strategies. The adult learner is generally less tolerant of a passive lecture format and eager to take responsibility for learning. There is a substantial body of research on lifelong and continuing education which encompasses everything from adult learner motivational theory to adult learning environments, including the narrower field of continuing professional education.

All higher education programmes should specify the learning outcomes that students will achieve in terms of:

i) knowledge and understanding
ii) key skills
iii) cognitive skills
iv) subject- or occupation-specific skills

All higher education programmes should incorporate the following four key skills:

i) communication
ii) information technology
iii) numeracy
iv) learning how to learn.

There are three different ways of addressing key skills when using the web for teaching and learning. One involves using the web as a vehicle for developing key skills, and a second involves being able to use the web as part of the key skill related to information technology. The third one is more complicated; there is an indirect learning gain that results from the key skill of 'learning how to learn', which can be achieved by students using technology independently in their studies.

In the development of IT-related key skills, the web obviously needs to play a role. With the increased use of the web for publication of information, there is also an increased need for academic graduates to be able to use the web effectively. An important part of learning to use the web is learning how to deal with the information it makes available, and how to judge the value and reliability of information the web provides.

These are the real information skills within information technology skills. Furthermore, it may be appropriate to learn how to record information on the web, through publishing web pages or by knowing how to contribuite to data bases. More and more resources are appearing on the web, helping students to develop their key skills.

When using technology an interesting, highly valuable side-effect occurs in student learning. The nature of using technology means that information, and the process of digesting information, go through a far more structured path than other transfers of information do. Learners react to this by organising their thoughts and their work processes in a far more structured way than they normally would.

Many institutions are turning to new technologies, especially the web, to provide student support. There are three main areas in which the web can play an important role in the delivery of student support:

i) Providing flexible study opportunities through online subject-related materials;

ii) Supporting students' study skills on the web;

iii) Providing new ways of student-tutor and student-student communication.

Web materials are used to support traditional courses and facilitate students' access to resources in a more flexible way. Basic IT skills are required for students to use web-based materials and, very often, to produce their own. Web materials are often used to help students—and staff—to make more effective use of their IT skills and to develop new information skills which will help them in their learning.

The materials include advice and tutorials on a widerange of topics such as using software applications, using IT facilities in classrooms, finding and managing information, presentation skills, essay writing, etc. Libraries are ideal partners in developing such materials, since they have expert knowledge of student needs with regard to information skills.

The use of Computer Assisted Instruction (CAI) in networked technology can be highly effective for the drill and practice of basic skills. It has now advanced to multimedia and networked technologies. It allows students to think analytically and critically and to work collaboratively. It supports a constructivist approach to education, and could be seen as driving educational reform in this way.

Research on the effectiveness of network technologies is not very extensive, but studies have shown increased proficiency levels in information-gathering, organising and presenting information, carrying out multimedia projects and obtaining help with basic skills. Network technologies can improve the roles of teachers and administrators by streamlining administrative tasks, thereby freeing up time for instruction and professional development. Isolation may also be decreased by the use of e-mail and the internet to communicate with colleagues, etc., and facilities such as distance education courses could increase professional development.

ONLINE INSTRUCTION

The term 'online instruction' refers to teaching and learning mediated by a computer. Online instruction implies a connection to a computer system at a venue distinct from the learner's personal computer; this venue can be across the world or across campus. Learning networks comprise professors and students communicating with each other in real time (synchronously) or off-line and sequentially (asynchronously).

Online teaching and learning occurs in a range of modes. Briefly, these modes, in order of an increasing computer component, are:

i) supplemental or adjunct,

ii) mixed, and

iii) wholly online.

While there are as many modes of instruction as there are varieties of students, let us attempt to generalise a few categories of each so that a number of options for online instruction can be fashioned and discussed within an orderly framework.

Let us generalise the instructional modes into four types: training, education toward an undergraduate degree, continuing education, and graduate work.

In training, a particular package of knowledge is imparted to an individual so that he or she can assume work within a system, as the firefighters do, for example. In becoming trained, an individual relinquishes autonomy. The purpose of education, as compared to training, is to impart autonomy to the student. In teaching students to think critically, we say in effect 'Student, know thyself'. Education is not just the transmission of knowledge, important as that is, but also has to do with the transformation of persons and the development of critical thinking skills.

John Dewey's theory of learning and growth fits neatly into place here. In a wide-ranging set of influential books and articles Dewey urges educators to think of learning as at once both social and cognitive. Persons do not learn, he argues, in the way that sponges absorb water. Persons are changed, however subtly, by everything they learn. Dewey captures a powerful image of liberal learning when he shows how an adequate learning theory must embody the education of the mind, body, emotions, and spirit.

Continuing education and lifelong learning are imprecise terms that might connote something as simple as a weeklong technical workshop or as extensive as a part-time advanced professional degree programme scheduled around a full-time job. The former example might be considered professional training, as in the case of a chemical engineer at an oil company who spends a week learning the practical intricacies of distillation tower design. Professional seminars or workshops can be developed from within the company, but can also be offered to private industry by a team of university faculty members.

Likewise for continuing education in the form of advanced degrees, students have already gained a great deal of socialisation through their first degree, and less of this is needed unless the student has switched fields and needs socialisation in the new field. In lieu of the socialising component, many graduate students must learn to perform research, and this learning component distinguishes graduate school from both undergraduate work and professional training. In many cases it may be argued that the nuances of a field and the performance of research within it must be learned under the personal mentorship of a research advisor. This need, as well as the actual performance of experimental research, greatly constrains the means of delivery of many types of graduate level work.

There are two main groups of students. The traditional student is young, full time or significantly part-time, and attends face-to-face classes. This category would include both two- and four-year institutions. It is with the traditional student that we associate the need for socialisation in college. A mature or nontraditional student might be older, working full time, and might already possess one or more degrees. By virtue of their state in life non-traditional students are more place-bound than traditional students, whether to a home in which children are cared for, or by a job location. This category also includes the "young" non-traditional student who is also place-bound, as for example, an advanced student at a small and understaffed rural high school who seeks an advanced course in college math or physics. In either case, though for different reasons, socialisation is not a requisite of the college level education that each of these students might receive at a distance. With the mature student, it has already occurred, and with the young student, it will occur at a later stage.

Table 6.1: Contexts for online instruction

Type of student	*Training*	*Education*	*Continuing Education*	*Graduate Education*
Traditional: young full time in-class	Vocational school, employee training	Associate, bachelor degrees	N.A	Masters, doctorate degrees with heavy research component
	Online modes: - adjunct - mixed	Online modes: - adjunct - mixed	Professional workshops, certifications	Online modes: - adjunct - mixed
Non-traditional place-bound part-time mature or young and place-bound	Vocational school, employee training	Associate, bachelor degrees individual courses of interest	Online mode: wholly online	Advanced degrees with lesser research component
	Online mode: wholly online	Online mode: wholly online		Online mode: wholly online

The varieties of students, modes of instruction, and corresponding options for online delivery can be generalised as in Table 6.1. Of course the categories in this table are by no means definitive; they have been formulated only to help with ensuing discussion. Seven areas have been delineated—four instructional modes and two types of students for each, excepting "traditional" continuing education which by definition does not occur.

Online teaching is not just for the non-traditional, place-bound student. Universities and education providers have began to realise that significant numbers of students subscribing to totally online courses are in fact to be found on-campus. Adjunct and mixed modes are possible and these by definition are available only in traditional settings.

Teaching a class without the ability to see and hear the students in person appears daunting. The enlightened, quizzical, or stony facial expressions, the sighs of distress or gasps of wonder, and even the less-than-subtle raised hands or interjected queries that constitute immediate feedback to a lecture, discussion, or clinical situation are absent. Yet the proponents of online instruction will argue that these obstacles can be overcome, and that the online format has its own advantages. The ability to sit and think as one composes a question or comment also can raise the quality of the discussion. In the hands of professors who know what they are doing, online instruction is superior to face-to-face instruction.

Unless the teacher facilitates the networking activities skillfully, serious problems may develop. A conference may turn into a monologue of lecture-type material to which very few responses are made. It may become a disorganised mountain of information that is confusing and overwhelming for the participants. It may even break down socially into name calling rather than building a sense of community. There are two related parts to this caution. First, the teaching paradigm must change for online instruction, away from the traditional lecture format. Second, the instructor has an important role in moderating the interaction.

The online environment is essentially a space for written interaction. This is its limitation and potential. Electronic networks should be appropriated with this in mind, and not turned into poor copies of the face-to-face classroom that they can never adequately reproduce.

The role of teacher as online "moderator" can be summarised in three parts: contextualising functions, monitoring functions, and meta-functions. The role of the first two functions is to compensate for the absence of physical cues found in a traditional classroom. Students must be explicitly told, for example, that the conference in which they are about to proceed is a "class" or a "meeting" or a support group. After a topic is introduced, students' comments must be monitored to assure that all are participating and that they understand the meeting mode. If CMC has both limitations and potential, these first two functions compensate for the limitations of this medium, while the third, meta functions, give rise to its potential.

Meta-communication, or communication about communication, has two parts. First, it is needed to resolve problems in communication that would be addressed in the classroom by body language or a request to speak up on the part of the students. Second, comments are needed which summarise the state of a discussion and provide a sense of accomplishment and direction. These are called "weaving" comments, and it is particularly with these that the class gets more deeply into themes than students in a face-to-face classroom.

The theory is constructivism which supports the text-based, collaborative learning paradigm of CMC, evolved earlier than and independently of CMC, but which has extensive applications in the use of computer supported collaborative learning tools. While there is no canonical form of constructivism, the theory involves the belief that better learning occurs when knowledge is the result of a situated construction of knowledge.

Online communication may enhance the goals and tactics of constructivist educational theory. One of the most significant is the development of flexible "scaffolding" for student work where the instructional design and teaching tactics surround, but do not fill in, the learning by students. A second factor concerns the importance of a distributed, or even global audience for student work which, connected with the student's ability to adapt to alternative roles, may fundamentally alter a student's view of their work. Finally, the archiving function of online technology may form the basis for new methods of student portfolio construction. Through all these points, online environments offer interesting opportunities for learning to take place through social interactions in areas where the individual's prior and emerging knowledge meet.

Evaluation of Online Instructional Effectiveness

A number of factors would seem to call for the evaluation of online learning effectiveness in comparison to traditional classes and programmes. One is certainly economic: the high cost for the technology and staff to support it. A second is pedagogic: implementers of novel teaching methods, and their administrators for that matter, are in need of feedback so that the quality of teaching can be maximised.

The introduction of new educational technologies, including computer networking, benefits from educational evaluation and assessment. Assessment includes both top-down accountability approaches (reporting of results for accountability purposes) and bottom-up instructional improvement (helping individual students gain most from instruction). Both perspectives share a common goal of improving education and are important at all stages of adopting technological innovations. However, the evaluation of online learning is not straightforward.

The new paradigms of online instruction call for new paradigms of evaluation. Formative feedback as well as summative evaluations should consider a multiplicity of evidence beyond written exercises and tests, for example, "participation by students in class discussions, project work, and individual and group interviews."

The key concept in network teaching is to facilitate collaborative learning, not to deliver a course in a fixed and rigid, one-way format.

i) Do not lecture.
ii) Be clear about expectations of the participants.
iii) Be flexible and patient.
iv) Be responsive.
v) Do not overload.
vi) Monitor and prompt for participation.
vii) For assignments, set up small groups and assign tasks to them.
viii) Be a process facilitator.
ix) Write weaving comments every week or two.
x) Organise the interaction.
xi) Set rules and standards for good netiquette.
xii) Establish clear norms for participation and procedures for grading.
xiii) Assign individuals or small groups to play the role of teacher and of moderator for portions of the course.
xiv) Close and purge moribund conferences in stages.
xv) Adopt a flexible approach toward curriculum integration on global networks.

The American Distance Education Consortium (ADEC) has set forth a concise set of guiding principles for distance teaching and learning. Their distance learning guidelines can be applied wholly to online learning:

i) The learning experience must have a clear purpose with tightly focused outcomes and objectives.

ii) The learner is actively engaged.

iii) The learning environment makes appropriate use of a variety of media.

iv) Learning environments must include problem-based as well as knowledge-based learning.

v) Learning experiences should support interaction and the development of communities of interest.

vi) The practice of distance learning contributes to the larger social mission of education and training in a democratic society.

REFERENCES

Barron, A., K. S., Ivers, and L., Sherry, "Exploring the Internet", *The Computing Teacher*, 22(2), 14-19, 1994.

Boshier, R., M. Wilson, and A., Qayyum, "Lifelong education and the World Wide Web: American hegemony or diverse utopia?" *International Journal of Lifelong* Education, Vo.l 18 (4) 275-285, 1999.

Cowham T., 'Information and Learning Technology: A Development Handbook' in FE Matters, February, 1997.

Ellsworth, J.H., *Education on the Internet*, Indianapolis: Sams Publishing, 1994.

Hancock, A. *Contemporary Information and Communication Technologies and Education. International Commission on Education for the 21 st Century*. UNESCO, 1993

Harasim, L. (ed.), *Online Education*, New York: Praeger, 1990.

Jonassen, D.H., "Applications and limitations of hypertext technology for distance learning", Paper presented at the Distance Learning Workshop, Armstrong Laboratory, San Antonio, TX, 1992.

Kerr, E., S., Hiltz, *Computer-Based Instruction*, 17(1), 1982.

Owston, R.D., "The World Wide Web, A Technology to Enhance Teaching and Learning?", *In Educational Researcher*, 26, 1997.

Portway, P., and C., Lane, *Technical Guide to Tele-conferencing and Distance Learning*, San Ramon, CA: Applied Business telecommunications, 1992.

Williams, M., and K., Paprock, Instructional design in distance education. *The ED Journal*, 7(4), 1994.

7

Open and Distance Learning: Educational Innovation

Distance learning has been in existence since the nineteenth century in the form of correspondence courses. Given that unbounded enthusiasm is usually reserved for new ideas that promise a brave new world and a panacea for all society's ills. The current rush to implement distance learning programmes by colleges and universities is occurring for three major reasons:

i) the convergence of communication and computing technologies,
ii) the need for information age workers to acquire new skills without interrupting their working lives for extended periods of time, and
iii) the need to reduce the cost of education.

The convergence of communication technologies is producing a plethora of hybrid technology products and services. These new products and services will soon permit widespread availability of diverse forms of information, education, services, and entertainment. Many of these products are able to address the difficult educational problems.

Open and distance learning is closely linked to innovation in information and communication technologies, to the identification of new learning needs and new ideas about how information may be accessed and applied in the information society. In particular open and distance learning has the potential to enhance a more student-centred and consumer-oriented approach to education, leading in turn to more extensive contact between educational institutions on the one hand and community-based organisations, business and industry on the other. Innovation in how resources are organised is essential, and open and distance learning has demonstrated how the labour (i.e., teacher) to capital (i.e., technology) ratio can be improved to lead to greater efficiency.

Unlike open and distance learning, conventional schools and universities are still organised on the assumption that learning is dependent on a single informed person imparting information by word of mouth to a small group of listeners in a classroom. A multitude of solitary individuals are responsible for the organisation and control of information, are designers of their courses, manage the instructional process, are testers, motivators, counsellors and evaluators for a handful of learners. Teaching, in other words, remains organised as a craft not a system.

With open and distance learning there is greater specialisation of labour and investment in capital to replace certain human activities. It is this different form of structure that makes the technology effective and leads to lowering costs while increasing access. To bring about this increased efficiency, new national policies and reforms in regulatory frameworks may be needed.

Many countries have already engaged in reform of their telecommunications policies, particularly regarding internet backbone development, and relaxation of the monopolies of publicly owned telecommunications companies. New international partnerships are emerging, not only of telecommunications providers, but also of universities and training institutions, equipment providers, content producers and publishers, software developers, assessment services, credit banks, and library services. However, the organisational frameworks in which technology is used in education have not been treated to the same radical policy reviews as has the telecommunications infrastructure itself. Other works have to be done to establish policies concerning international trade in educational services and such related matters as institutional accreditation and assessment, certification of learning, intellectual property rights, and incentive structures.

As teachers become less information communicators and more knowledge processors, experts in learning rather than content, so technology can help them do their jobs more efficiently provided they are organised into better integrated systems. Since the economies of large-scale production enable distance education systems to invest larger sums in the design and development of learning materials than smaller, conventional teaching institutions, the quality of such materials is usually higher, and this in turn makes for a raising of standards throughout the educational system. This may have a particularly important influence when teachers and professors of conventional institutions become involved in the development or use of these materials, for instance on contract with a distance teaching institution.

The potential of distance learning to increase innovation and creativity in conventional education depends on the degree of interaction between distance learning systems and conventional systems. Ideally, there ought to be formal links between such institutions and the conventional system, in order that they may serve as national resource centres.

A new organisational model is that of a network of institutions and individuals that together provide the kind of services delivered by single mode institutions, but on a more flexible and open basis through a process of commissioning. A small management team is one of two essential requirements for a network; and the other is a significant funding resource that allows the management team to obtain the quality resources needed from wherever they are located. This approach promises a very flexible, versatile, responsive system that produces high quality without commitment to ongoing institutional costs, and delivers efficiently by employing the comparative advantage of each institution in a region.

Another innovative model is the Independent Study model, which gives learners control of their own learning programmes through use of new technology. This calls for a different type of organisation than was useful when information was stored centrally in a location to which students could travel, or in a distance teaching centre from which they it could be distributed. Such an organisation could make instructors anywhere available to students anywhere, and could make courses prepared by any institution available to students anywhere.

GENERATIONS OF DISTANCE LEARNING

The world's first university distance learning programme is said to have been offered through an extension division from the University of Chicago in 1892 under the direction of William Rainey Harper. In the US, the use of correspondence courses increased significantly after World War II when many veterans hurried to complete the education they had missed while in service. What distinguishes correspondence learners is their characteristic self-motivation and discipline, and their ability to learn by reading and writing rather than listening and speaking.

Distance learners in correspondence courses miss the opportunity of social interaction and learning from other students. Additionally, the evaluation of the learning must also be written, which rules out performance, practical, and team evaluations. With correspondence courses, the "instruction" must be converted from lecture notes and other materials into a purely written form, a time-consuming process that some instructors find difficult. However, the bottom line is that correspondence courses are the oldest and most cost-effective method of distance education for both the student and the education institution.

Communication technologies provide one-way, two-way, or multiple-way communication, whether the 'ways' are broadband or narrowband, and whether the return rate is fast or slow. For example, the postal service can be broadband carrying print, audio, and video-tapes, but the return rate can be painfully slow. The telephone is a good technology for two-way audio conferencing, but it has no visual elements. If one is having an audioconference, any visual supporting material must be on site for all participants. The rapid deployment of the fax machine has facilitated effective audioconferencing by supplying the visual component.

Technologies predominantly used in distance learning in the early and mid-twentieth century have been primarily broadband in one direction—fitting the educational model of information transfer from faculty to student. The printed page or the radio or television "talking head" took on the role of the lecturer in transferring information to the students. This delivery mode did not generally incorporate any two-way interaction among students, and provided minimal interaction between the faculty and the student. Another drawback of this generation of technology is that television is also used primarily as a family or group entertainment or news medium. It can be difficult for students to shift from an entertainment mindset to an active learning mode. A related constraint of some of the traditional broadband one-way technologies was their time dependency. Many of these programmes were broadcast only once or twice and a student had to be listening or watching at those specific times.

The advent of the VCR and cable channel proliferation have made these one-way technologies more flexible and forgiving of people's schedules, enabling timeshifting of the broadcast portion of the telecourses. They also enable the alternative of bypassing broadcast completely by making the content available on video-tapes that can be sent to the student and used at any time.

Computer-based education (CBE) came into existence in the 1980s. CBE materials are powerful in the interaction and simulation richness that they can provide and thus represent a major technological advancement. These materials best support the dialogue between students and resources, and when future advancements are complete, they will effectively support collaboration between students. Another major constraint of the broadband one-way technologies is the difficulty of creating a meaningful relationship between a faculty member and isolated students, or of developing a community of learners among the faculty and possible cohort of students.

The technologies of the third and fourth generations electronic mail, chat rooms, bulletin boards, desktop videoconferencing, and interactive two-way videoconferencing now make possible the development of learning communities across time and distance. Especially valuable to distance education was the emergence of two-way videoconferencing classroom technologies. Videoconferencing has grown in sophistication such that classrooms can be used as remote sites to send or receive scheduled instruction. Videoconferencing technologies enable real two-way audio/video communication. These technologies are finally becoming more affordable and easier to operate.

Virtual classrooms can be created that consist of one or many classrooms. A virtual classroom might be composed of two classrooms many miles apart linked by a T1 line (point-to-point) or of many classrooms linked by a video bridge and multiple T1 lines (multipoint to multipoint). If the virtual classroom consists of only two classrooms, a videoconferencing class can be initiated by a simple call placed between the two classroom videoconferencing units. This technology requires video codecs (compression- decompression) units sold by companies such as British Telecom, CLI, PicTEL, and VTEL. Currently the costs for these codecs are significant. Low-end, small-room videoconferencing can be accomplished using relatively economical adapted classrooms for sending and receiving video. A high-end, studio-quality classroom will also have professional cameras, operators, and monitors.

New developments such as CU-SeeMe and QuickTime (videoconferencing software products) are bringing video-conferencing to the desktop level. Thus, in designing distance education programmes, three levels of video-conferencing can be considered:

i) desktop videoconferencing for faculty-to-student and student-to-student discussion and collaboration;
ii) small conference rooms for instruction and collaboration between small groups; and
iii) large classroom studios for large group regular instruction.

The primary differentiating feature between the distance learning technologies of today and those of previous generations is the capability for timely and personal interaction, the basis of most satisfying relationships. Technologies today allow the delivery of distance learning programmes almost anytime, anywhere. Today's technologies enable synchronous communications across long distances and with large groups, providing the perception of "almost being there" no matter where one is. New categories of media events are evolving—online interactive interviews with rock stars, for example.

With technologies that allow rapid-response, asynchronous communication, a student can post a question for a faculty member or other students and receive a reply sometimes in minutes. This capability also creates new communication patterns and expectations. A faculty member can manage a course using a variety of social and intellectual spaces on the network. New technologies also enable faculty, students, and support staff to handle all recruiting, admission, registration and fees, and student life online.

Successful distance learning students generally have the skills to be independent learners, and are comfortable in the realm of textual materials. Most students with this set of characteristics tend to be mature adults. The young adult who was not successful in high school does not fit this profile. Student maturity will always be an important indicator of success in learning, but it will be less important in the future. The new distance-learning technologies enable faculty to hold meetings, stay in touch, provide structure, and provide frequent response and interaction. They enable faculty or support staff who have the time to give some much-needed guidance, encouragement, and hand-holding to students who need such help.

In the early 1900s the student was commonly viewed as an empty vessel into which the faculty member "poured" knowledge. In this model, the faculty member was the "one who knew all" and students came to the faculty member with a yearning to know what the faculty member knew. With this philosophy the goal of distance learning was to "get the knowledge content" out to the student. So the curriculum designers analysed the knowledge content, divided it into manageable chunks, and structured readings to teach the knowledge objectives in these chunks. This sounds like a reasonable approach.

Today's view of the student is quite different, and it is reasonable to say that students are qualitatively different as well. The understanding of the teaching and learning process is more advanced, and we know that the students need to be actively processing and integrating information for learning to occur. The focus is changing for the curriculum designers as well. Designers still must analyse the knowledge content and determine appropriately sized chunks; but designers must also analyse the skills to be developed and incorporate complex real-world problems into the content materials. Students may bring applied knowledge to the teaching and learning event that is new to the faculty member. In these cases, the role of the faculty member changes from the font of all knowledge to the mentor who helps to interpret information in the light of the discipline and a more comprehensive perspective. For effective learning today, designers must plan for interactive, collaborative events among faculty, students, and other resources.

Over the past 20 years, the transformation of a relatively simple computer network used by a few researchers into a global internet, involving hundreds of millions of people and generating a new economic order, took government, business and education, by surprise. Given the well-established tendency for people to underestimate the extent and rate of technological change, it seems reasonable to suggest that the extent to which the internet created economic and social upheaval in the past 20 years is likely to pale into insignificance by comparison with the changes occurring in the next decade. The next few years will encompass the significant impact of broadband, wireless, smart cars, smart fridges, streaming media, voice recognition and the inevitable growth of new internet applications.

For many years, universities with a significant commitment to distance and open education institutions have been at the forefront of adopting new technologies to increase access to education and training opportunities. Distance education operations have evolved through the following four generations:

i) the correspondence model based on print technology;
ii) the multimedia model based on print, audio and video technologies;
iii) the telelearning model, based on applications of telecommunications technologies to provide opportunities for synchronous communication; and
iv) the flexible learning model based on online delivery via the internet.

Although many universities are just beginning to implement fourth generation distance education initiatives, the fifth generation is already emerging based on the further exploitation of new technologies. The fifth generation of distance education is essentially a derivation of the fourth generation, which aims to capitalise on the features of the internet and the web. To place the fifth generation intelligent flexible learning model into a meaningful conceptual framework, it is first worth reviewing briefly certain features of the previous four generations of distance education.

Some of the characteristics of the various models of distance education that are relevant to the quality of teaching and learning are summarised in Table 7.1.

Table 7.1: Models of distance education delivery technologies

First generation	
Model:	The correspondence model
Media:	Print
Second generation	
Model:	The multimedia model
Media:	Print
	Audio-tape
	Video-tape
	Computer-based learning (e.g., CML/CAL/IMM)
	Interactive video (disc and tape)
Third generation	
Model:	The telelearning model
Media	Audio-teleconferencing
	Videoconferencing
	Audiographic communication
	Broadcast TV/Radio
	Audio-teleconferencing
Fourth generation	
Model:	The flexible learning model
Media	Interactive multimedia (IMM) online
	Internet-based access to WWW resources
	Computer-mediated communication
Fifth generation	
Model:	The intelligent flexible learning model
	Interactive multimedia (IMM) online
	Internet-based access to WWW resources
	Computer-mediated communication, using automated response systems
	Campus portal access to institutional processes and resources

Through the development and implementation of: automated courseware production systems, automated pedagogical advice systems, and automated business systems, the fifth generation of distance education has the potential to deliver a quantum leap in economies of scale and associated cost-effectiveness. Further, effective implementation of fifth generation distance education technology is likely not only to transform distance education, but also to transform the experience of on campus students.

The new generation of distance learning programmes use a broad mix of techniques, methodologies, and media. As in other areas of society, a new educational technology does not necessarily replace an old one. A more common scenario is that the new technology takes its place among the range of technologies for meeting a particular set of needs. Or a general technology may have an extended phasing-in period and then settle in for a long period of serving a small niche. The radio is a good example of a technology that was used for distance learning when it was the only technology widely accessible. The mix of media to be used in designing distance learning programmes has become very complex as the technologies have expanded.

In the case of the early generations of distance learning the infrastructure requirements for student support consisted of what we now view as fairly straightforward technologies: the postal service, radio, television, and audio-cassettes. The list of infrastructure requirements for distance learning programmes based on computers, computer networking, databases of digital information, and the internet is daunting.

Curriculum designers must know what resources students will have access to while they design distance learning programmes. Research data on the number of students who currently have access to computers support a view that the critical mass of dissemination has been reached and that it is only a matter of time before computer technology, including access to the internet, is widespread. While designers cannot assume access today for all populations of students, many distance learning programmes are moving forward by making computer and computer network access a prerequisite for participating in certain distance learning programmes, and other colleges and universities are beginning to require all on-campus students to have their own computers, with the institution providing the network access.

The ICTs offer an opportunity to close the gap between the effectiveness of the experiences of on-campus students and those of distance learning students. The world wide web and the internet and the infrastructure of fibre, cable, and phone lines now offer real-time, 30-frame-per-second, two-way audio and video communications. With these technologies readily available to at least 10 per cent of the population, it is time to rethink the role of distance education in higher education.

The following strategies may help to address the three major challenges—quality, access, and cost—confronting higher education today:

i) Don't try to teach more, but rather devise venues for learning that take advantage of the technology revolution.
ii) Devise multiple programme types that support shortened time-to-degree, smaller and more modular courses, and more extensive use of self-paced, immersion learning software resources.
iii) Reach out to learners rather than bring them to campus. This can increase productivity and reduce or contain cost.

All of these strategies can be used to meet the needs of both campus and off-campus learners.

The traditional mission of education institutions has included the creation, dissemination, and preservation of knowledge. Global alliances and partnerships among colleges and universities are essential if the goal of teaching universal knowledge is to be attainable in the information age. As we are beginning to understand, building such partnerships, at some level, is critical to an institution's well-being and future. Distance learning programmes, if well supported and delivered, will also enable colleges and universities to forge close bonds with their students throughout their lifetimes. The emerging new teaching and learning paradigm will affect our institutions in significant ways. In addition to rethinking our missions, it is time to rethink education and distance learning in the light of new technologies.

The dialogues which serve as the foundation of instructional strategies and practices are: the dialogue between the faculty and the students, the dialogue between and among students, and the dialogue between a student and instructional resources such as books, films, reference materials, research data, and experts. The array of communication and computing technologies now available are powerful enablers of these dialogues. For example, the dialogue between the faculty and students might be facilitated via:

i) Two-way interactive audio/video delivered to multiple sites.
ii) Real-time (synchronous) or delayed (asynchronous) classroom lectures which students might access across high-speed multimedia networks from home, from work, or from anywhere.
iii) Online electronic discussions, one on one or one to many, including desktop conferencing advising sessions. Intensive synchronous on-site seminars or institutes, similar to what we offer in continuing education for professionals.
iv) Fireside chats accompanied by beverages (fill in your favourite), cheese, and crackers.
v) Electronic mail, chat facilities, bulletin boards, online help, etc., are excellent and effective low-cost vehicles for integrating interactive dialogue into what were predominantly one-way distance-learning models.

Giving faculty these tools together with assistance in instructional design regarding how to integrate these into their distance learning courses and their on-campus courses can give a needed boost to the quality and satisfaction of teaching and learning models.

The key change in the teaching and learning paradigm of the future will be the single most significant change to occur in education in hundreds of years. This is the move away from the physical classroom as the "framework for interaction" or the "gathering place", to the world wide web as the point of departure for a learning experience. Websites are now as easy to develop as word-processed documents. Support may be needed for the linking and the internet placement, but the web is becoming a friendly place to see and be seen. It is a good place for the faculty member to introduce himself or herself to new cohorts of learners; it is a place where much of the normal communication of a course can be conducted. The web is also the place where much of the dialogue between and among faculty and students can occur. Some of these dialogues will be synchronous and others will be asynchronous.

It is an easy leap to see that our campus buildings in the future may look and feel much more like a combination of today's television production studios and conference centres. People will come together for longer periods of "class time" for specific goals and objectives that truly cannot be met in any other way. Despite the rapid pace of technology and the ability to move digital bits rather than people across geographic distances, people will still want to come together occasionally for events and hand-shaking and hugging.

With a move to wide-scale use of interactive strategies and materials in higher education and offering of courses in virtual space and time, instructional design becomes more critical to ensure quality of outcomes. Faculty are generally unconsciously competent in instructional design. They are competent in that they have been designing instruction for years; they are unconscious in that they cannot articulate the principles of instructional design. This situation is not particularly troublesome as long as the environment in which they are teaching does not change significantly and they are available to correct any misconceptions. However, change the environment and their teaching role, and it becomes critical that faculty develop knowledge of instructional design or, alternatively, be supported in instructional design in some way.

Many students come to a higher education institution with the primary purpose of becoming certified. In this regard, the students share the expectations of the larger society that needs certified people who are competent practitioners and theoreticians of certain bodies of knowledge. When we know the desired outcomes of education, and when we can measure those outcomes, we can be comfortable requiring individuals to pass a competency test, such as a driver's test, real estate appraisal test, etc.

When the desired outcomes are a set of complex cognitive, behavioural, and attitudinal skills, we have traditionally turned to a time-based model of education, with a measure of competency exams at regular intervals. This model says the following: We are not quite certain about the exact nature of the educational outcomes, and we are not quite certain how to measure these outcomes, but the students need to develop a very complex and rich set of skills and experience.

Traditionally, if students have spent a certain amount of "time on task" with appropriate interaction with knowledgeable faculty and resources and performance on faculty exams, students have generally performed the expected tasks in society in an acceptable fashion. In the higher education and professional arenas, we often require a time-based experience coupled with a competency-based demonstration—the bar exam, the nursing exam, and so forth. In other fields, we combine a time-based experience with a set of products, such as the series of innovative research projects required for a Ph.D. in science, or a portfolio of art or writings.

We can design distance learning courses from the viewpoint of a time-based model or a competency-based model, or some combination of these two. In practice, most courses, including distance learning courses, are designed with a blend of these two models. However, it is important to differentiate the assumptions behind the two as we move into distance learning experiences. State regulations and accreditation models that specify a certain number of required "contact hours" for a three-credit undergraduate course, for example, assume a bias toward a time-based model. But, a dominantly time-based model focuses on an element that is often irrelevant to the specified outcomes. The time-based model does have a certain amount of validity because we know that learning requires time, but regulations based on time regulate outcomes indirectly and superficially.

Most faculty and instructional designers begin planning for a course by specifying a structured body of knowledge for a semester. A concurrent step is to specify the desired student outcomes. This is the competency-based approach merged with the time-based model. Given this context, here are some of the principles or guidelines that might be adopted for designing interactive distance learning courses:

i) Interactive distance learning courses will be designed based on the core instructional design questions listed above so that the learning is focused on outcomes appropriate to the student and societal needs. These activities will be designed to build skills and relationships appropriate to each student's continuity of learning growth.

ii) Interactive distance learning courses will use a set of multiple communications media to enable and encourage active and collaborative learning. This means that interactive distance learning courses will use video, audio, electronic mail and communications, the world wide web, online seminars, and content resources as appropriate for the goals and objectives of the learning, the characteristics of the students, and available resources.

iii) A three-credit course is generally assumed to be 135 hours. On-campus courses now assume 45 contact hours. The remaining 90 hours is generally considered to be study time - either individually or in a group using a variety of content resources, such as books, journals, doing research, and simply learning content. This design will be translated into the context of a combination of competency and time-based models.

iv) Interactive distance learning course design will be based on the principle that the core of education is dialogue and communication, and that balancing the use of the three dialogues—faculty to student, student to student, and student to resources—generally promotes an effective learning experience.

For each body of defined knowledge, there is a set of core concepts and principles that need to be learned, then acted upon or manipulated or applied in some way, and finally used in complex problem solving. To support this type of interactive learning, we need to be developing the kinds of resources that facilitate these types and levels of learning experience. For example, online reference materials, CD-ROMs, and databases, in addition to books, are needed for the basic learning of concepts.

Comprehensive, multi-layered discipline and interdisciplinary databases are needed to accommodate the experiences students need for various levels of content interaction and application. We need materials that offer real-life scenarios and situations requiring complex problem-solving skills. In many areas, this might mean complex simulations; in others, internships addressing real problems. These needs can also support the needs of society for more skilled resources to solve real problems.

The conservatory approach to learning has been a grand tradition in the arts; we now are at a point where we should be establishing regular internships and conservatories in other fields as well.

Today's computing and communication technologies cannot be adopted in a piecemeal fashion. They require change at the systemic and institutional level. The roles of students, faculty, and administrators are changing; the roles of our institutions are changing—even expanding if institutions so choose. The needs are so great that additional private institutions will be established to target certain market segments.

We are starting to see some of these new systems emerging now. We need new institutional processes, new support structures, and new teaching and learning resources.

Many of the trends now occurring in higher education are symptomatic of these large systemic changes on the horizon. These trends can help to provoke our thoughts about higher education in the twenty-first century. Some of these trends include:

i) Credit transfer mechanisms, credit banks, identification, and accreditation for prior learning experiences are making steady progress toward acceptability.

ii) Effectiveness and efficiency are expected outcomes of distance learning programmes and increasingly of all academic programmes.

iii) Student support systems are being recognised as crucial to learner success—wherever the learner may be.

iv) High-visibility distance learning courses, rigorously developed, are having a spin-off effect on teaching practices in conventional courses.

v) Expectations are growing for broad-based, learner-centered, cooperative/collaborative relationships across educational sectors.

vi) Production-line, industrialised distance learning models are being replaced by open learning models that respond to the students' needs for access, flexibility, a variety of learning strategies, and effective support systems.

A few institutions are testing and prototyping new contemporary learning environments, as a way of more rapidly defining and shaping the emerging new teaching and learning paradigm. The demands of education are too great to be met by our old models. We need to design a new teaching and learning paradigm that leverages and fits the power of the technology and the demands of our society where knowledge is expanding at an ever-increasing rate, and people need just-in-time learning and other expert and performance support systems.

CHANGING STRATEGICAL NEEDS

Open learning opens up new and increased opportunities for learning. Although different from other learning programmes, open learning contains nothing unfamiliar. It simply combines existing teaching media and techniques in a new and effective way. In developing countries, there is general concern on whether higher education still provides high quality learning.

Internationally, as in South Africa, there is a definite trend towards mixed mode education. It is not expected that more distance or open higher education institutions will be established, but that mixed mode education will most likely become the route to be followed. As a result of its telecommunication and technological infrastructure, SA is better placed than many developing countries, and it will have to judge for itself, what mix of technologies will be best suited for its particular circumstances. A national credit transfer system, as well as an open learning system with limited prescriptions are on the cards for SA.. This kind of educational intervention is the focus of a great deal of attention in South Africa.

Open learning is not reserved only for special groups, such as part-time adult learners, or the disadvantaged. It is not a thin educational experience, delivered to learners deprived of those interactions supposedly normal in conventional methodologies. Achievement is not measured in terms of where students study, the rate or pace at which they study, or the sequence in which they study, but instead by assessing as directly as possible the achievement of learning goals.

Open learning is a state of mind, an approach taken to the planning, design, preparation and presentation of courses by tutors, as well as the selection and use of learning strategies and associated resources by learners. It enables adult learners to take responsibility for their own learning: choices concerning what to learn and how to learn it, taking the initiative, while being supported by professional teachers, trainers, peers and employers.

Learners are encouraged to articulate their own learning needs and to translate these into a learning plan, where they study at a pace that suits their needs and abilities. Open learning implies that both tutors and learners need to be aware of the competence objectives which they are working towards, and the criteria for their achievement. In this respect, individual guidance and support are recognised as forming a part of support-learning. It allows learners to sign on for a course or programme at any point in the calendar year, through a roll-on, roll-off facility. Learners are provided with the opportunity to learn when they want (timing, frequency, duration), how they want (lecture, seminar, project, mediation, or reading), what they want (by being helped to define what constitutes learning to them).

The system permits students to start, stop and learn at their own pace, consistent with learner short- and long-range goals, situations and characteristics. Learners are involved in the assessment of their own learning, specifically in terms of negotiating criteria and methods by which assessment takes place. The interpretation of open as "free from restrictions" makes it necessary to expect of open learning institutions an absence of rigid entrance requirements, with the decisive factor for enrolment being student motivation and individual decision; and freedom for tutors and learners to decide within various parameters on study goals, content, method and assessment procedures.

Where distance education refers mainly to a mode of edelivery, distinguishing it from campus-based learning, open learning refers to structural changes. A distance education institution can also be an open institution, but not necessarily so, as the latter institution implies unimpeded access to study facilities, as well as avoidance of restrictions on free learning opportunities.

Distance education strategies—and associated expertise, systems and courseware (learning materials in any medium or combinations of media)—can make major contributions to the educationally effective and cost-effective implementation of an open approach.

Adult learners provide the opportunity for the work and community based learning that employers and community groups require. They can be combined in many different and flexible ways with other strategies, so as best to meet identified needs in identified circumstances.

Distance education that is based on quality courseware and learner support, offers an opportunity to reflect and underpin required standards. The courseware will offer learners and providers of education and training the opportunity to combine units of learning in different ways to meet different needs, an approach that is essential to achieve flexible pathways through higher education.

Quality distance education offerings are based on a close link between the identification of outcomes and the processes to assess whether those outcomes have been achieved. Quality distance education provision offers alternative access to education and training, at recognised standards, for those seeking individual fulfilment through lifelong recurrent education, who see distance education as their only chance for further and higher learning.

Further to this, distance education strategies can be combined with other learning strategies in innovative and flexible ways that exploit old and new technologies, on and off-campus learning (mixed mode education), on and off-the job learning (for employees who wish to use distance education to meet their own company-based training needs), guided and self-directed learning, in ways that not only offer increased access, but better and more relevant learning.

The potential of distance education for a whole range of flexible applications, its capacity to spread limited expertise and resources far beyond their point of origin, and the economies of scale of courseware and programmes, combine to offer cost-effective solutions to increased demands being made on the education and training resources of South Africa and other developing countries.

The emphasis on regular outcomes based assessment of quality distance education not only provides the means of standards related assessment within courses of study. It also provides a basis for the diagnostic assessment that is necessary to provide meaningful recognition of prior learning (RPL) and articulation between different sectors of education and training. There is a fundamental shift in the perception and practice of distance education as having the potential to establish and facilitate critical communities of learners at a distance.

Learning communities, which support the development of critical thinking skills, can be created at a distance, and they provide a mechanism for improving the quality of higher level distance education. This provides distance education students with the opportunity to participate in communities of inquiry, where they can consider alternatives, construct meaning, discuss discrepancies and develop consensual knowledge.

How distance educators view learning and particularly the role of social interaction in learning (on which learning communities are based), will be implicit in the design and delivery of the teaching-learning transaction at a distance. The opportunities for partnerships between experts in distance education from one organisation and subject experts from another, are well proven in other countries.

In South Africa, it has strong possibilities in the form of partnerships between distance education providers and centres of technical and academic excellence in other institutions, industry and professional areas. Partnerships with providers of facilities and technology related services, will offer even greater opportunities for flexible delivery of education and training to increased numbers of learners.

The most powerful partnerships will be between education providers and local communities. These will give learners and their communities meaningful involvement in, and a sense of ownership of, their learning and the facilities and resources that support it.

COST-EFFECTIVENESS OF ODL

Open and distance learning systems are oftenly more cost-efficient than other forms of education. Their cost structures are quite different from that in conventional types of education. The costs of open and distance learning vary a great deal according to the use of learning materials, media and technologies, and types and organisation of student support services. In order to evaluate costs it is also necessary to consider the rate of completion of studies.

Comparison of the average cost per student in open and distance learning institutions with that in broadly comparable traditional institutions operating in the same jurisdiction shows that the former is not always the most cost-efficient option. For example, table 1 shows the efficiency ratio (defined as the average cost per student in a distance teaching institution divided by the average cost per student in a conventional system) for a number of projects. An efficiency ratio of less than 1.0 means that the distance system is cheaper than the comparator tradition system; an efficiency ratio of more than 1.0 means that the average cost per student in the distance system is higher than that in a traditional system. Open and distance learning is not necessarily the most cost-efficient approach—but then there is no reason why it necessarily should be. Distance education methods may be the only way to reach some target audiences, in which case lowering the cost of education will not necessarily be an objective.

Table 7.2: Comparative costs of selected distance and traditional education projects

Project	*Comparator institution*	*Year*	*Efficiency ratio*
Instituto de Radiodifusao Educativa da Bahia (IRDEB), Brazil	Conventional school	1977	4.36
Malawi Correspondence College	Conventional day school	1977/1978	0.62
	Boarding school	1977/1978	0.23
Telesecundaria, Mexico	State day secondary school	1975	0.76
		1981	1.09
		1988	1.32
Centros APEC de Enseñanza a Distancia, Dominican Republic	Secondary level day school	1988	0.46
Tanzania Teacher Training at a distance	Face-to-face two-year trained teacher	1993	0.23
Universitas Terbuka teaching diploma programme, Indonesia	Traditional teacher training	1988	0.60
Allama Iqbal Open University, Pakistan	Traditional university	1988	0.22
University of the Air, Japan—recurrent costs, liberal arts programme	National universities	1986	0.47
	Public universities	1986	0.55
	Private universities day programme	1986	0.82
	Correspondence programme	1986	7.64
Abbey National, UK — training costs per trainee	Abbey National, traditional training costs	1990	0.42
Delco Electronics, UK — training costs per trainee	Delco Electronics traditional training costs	1990	1.08

However, the fact that open and distance learning may lower the costs of education is seen as one of its advantages, and the expectation that this will be the case has been a specific policy objective in a number of instances. While a particular form of open and distance learning may be cheaper than some options, it may actually be more expensive than other options The comparative cost of different systems may change over time.

Intuitively, in open and distance learning one would expect the cost per student to fall as economies of scale are achieved, yet in this particular case it rose. This was because the Telesecundaria was steadily reaching out to more and more disadvantaged communities, to set up schools with smaller and smaller class populations.

When comparing the costs of open and distance learning with those of more traditional face-to-face approaches, one needs to bear in mind that there are a range of factors that can affect the costs of traditional education, including staff: student ratios, the balance of 'big' group to 'little' group teaching, and the balance between time spent in class and in independent study and resource-based learning approaches.

At the higher education level, efficiencies in class-sizes, coupled with increased use of independent and resource-based learning strategies, have transformed the economics of the campus to support the view that mass higher education systems have a quite different economy from that of elite systems. Much of the increased productivity of education within the campus has derived from the conscious or unconscious adoption of methods used within open and distance learning in the campus setting.

The remarkable growth in the number of dual-mode institutions offering, in addition to face-to-face classes, flexible learning while by no means confined to the recent past, is part of this phenomenon. There are those who believe that the marginal costs of adding a flexible learning capability to traditional higher education is not only a cheaper option than setting up a new distance learning system, but delivers a wider curriculum choice.

However, traditional campus-based institutions, along with distance teaching institutions, have begun to use the internet to provide online courses. This has resulted in yet further changes in the costs and cost structure of educational provision, which are still being investigated. However, the indications are that many of the cost factors involved in online learning have been underestimated. A very great deal will depend upon the actual circumstances, and on the nature of the comparator institutions. Although distance education approaches often enable planners and managers to achieve greater efficiencies, there is a range of factors in play that will influence this outcome one way or the other.

Not all cost studies take account of the cost of completion, but in general, because the level of dropout tends to be higher in open and distance learning systems than in comparable face-to-face situations, the former tends to be less cost-efficient when measured by the average cost per graduate measure than is the case when it is measured by the average cost per student measure.

A range of factors may affect the cost-efficiency of particular distance learning systems. These include:

i) the number of learners enrolled;
ii) the size of the curriculum;
iii) the number of years over which courses are offered without change;
iv) containment of course development costs;
v) sharing course development costs;
vi) technology choice;
vii) the level of student support; and
viii) a range of working, labour market and structural practices.

The number of learners enrolled. The greater the enrolment, the more the fixed administrative costs of the system, and the resources invested in developing the curriculum and learning materials, will be spread across the student population, thus bringing down the unit cost of per student. However, the nature of the cost structure is such that most of the economies of scale are reaped at an early stage. As student numbers rise, so the gain in efficiency falls. Moreover, scale may bring its own complexities with the result that costs per student may actually begin to rise.

The size of the curriculum. The broader the curriculum on offer, the more courses will need to be offered, and the greater the volume of course materials that will need to be developed. The cost per student will therefore rise unless the increase in the number of courses is compensated for by an increase in the number of students.

The number of years over which courses are offered without change. One of the advantages of capturing knowledge in text, audio, video or computerised formats is that the material then exists as a more or less permanent record, and can be used again and again to teach successive cohorts of students. It makes economic sense to reuse the materials from year to year, so that the cost of developing the materials can be spread over more and more years. However, this can prove to be a drawback if the format does not allow for easy changes to be made to the materials, and if once the course is launched it becomes clear that poor initial design leads to the need to revise the course materials. To avoid this possibility, materials may be developmentally tested before they are produced in bulk.

A further problem is that the more years the materials are used, the greater the danger that they will become outdated. This is likely to be more serious in some subjects (e.g., computing, social sciences, education) than in others (basic maths, history). The extent to which this is a serious problem or not is to some extent affected by the approach taken to the design of the courses, and the ease with which changes can be made to materials. Modularisation of the materials' format, and the use of electronic formats, can make revision that much easier. Indeed, one of the advantages of online course formats is that development is no longer seen as a pre-presentation stage in the lifecycle of a course, but as something that happens continuously.

Containment of course development costs. The range of materials to be developed can be reduced by using existing textbooks in conjunction with wrap-around materials — materials that act as a commentary on a commercially produced textbook. This will reduce the costs of developing and producing course materials. This is certainly an option where the target population is capable of learning independently, but it may work less well with less experienced learners who tend to benefit from more structured and integrated materials.

Sharing course development costs. Another approach is to try to share the costs of developing course materials. One way is to design the materials so that they can be published in book form. This approach, often undertaken in partnership with a commercial publisher, generates income from sales that can then be used to offset the cost of developing and producing the materials. However, the income from royalties on sales to the public is usually relatively small. Another approach is to enter an agreement with another institution to share the development effort. In theory collaborative course development is an excellent way of reducing costs; in practice such collaboration can often be very difficult to get off the ground. Finally, it may be possible to buy in materials that have been produced by another distance teaching institution. Again, while in theory an attractive proposition, the rights charged for use of such materials can be significant, and there is some evidence that unless the number of copies required is relatively low, it can be cheaper to develop courses in house.

Technology choice: The range of media and technology employed in distance education is widening day by-day. Each technology has its own cost structure, so the choice of technology has an impact on the costs of the system. The cost of a given technology will depend on the equipment used, the running costs of the technology, and the labour costs involved in the development, production and delivery of materials carried by the technology. The costs of developing and producing materials in any given media varies enormously for all kinds of reasons, and so it is very difficult to make any categorical statements about the relative cost of media.

The move towards online education has provided an opportunity for course designers to shift away from the preparation of prepared materials towards less structured course formats in which much of the content is developed through student dialogue. This has radical implications for course costs, and for distance education it represents a shift away from capital in the form of learning materials back towards a more labour-intensive form of teaching unless it is accompanied by increased learner autonomy.

Education economists expect new information and communication technologies to have an impact on the productivity of educational services, but the costs of hardware, software and consumables are linked to the price structures of the supplier country, and not to local price structures. While the largely supplier-determined cost per learning hour using a computer may be less than the cost per learning hour with a teacher in developed countries, it is more expensive than the comparable cost in countries where labour costs are low, and where, as a consequence, the per hour/per pupil cost of teacher-based education is low.

The level of student support. Successful distance education systems require three elements: excellent teaching materials, efficient logistical systems, and responsive and where appropriate individualised student support systems. The difficulty with this is that the cost of student support tends to be driven by the number of students in the system, so that the absolute cost of providing student services increases rapidly with increases in student numbers. Moreover, student services are a direct student cost, so that the more that one spends on this, the less likely it is that the distance education option will prove to be cheaper than traditional education.

Working practices. Working practices can affect costs significantly. Courses that take students many hours to study tend to require more materials, and the range of materials on such courses is often such that several people will be required to develop the materials. Course teams, in which overall responsibility for content and teaching strategy is vested in a team rather than the individuals, have proved to be an effective but costly approach to course design. Reducing the transaction costs of team working by having a series of quasi-independent authors working under the direction of an academic editor will reduce costs.

Many distance teaching systems, faced with the need to support many hundreds or thousands of students studying course materials developed by a small team of academics, have divided the academic task between those who develop the materials, and those who support the students' learning. Further divisions of labour may occur where different individuals are appointed to mark examination scripts, and to provide general advice and educational guidance to the students. Such specialisation of tasks requires very considerable planning and management if it is to work effectively.

Generally distance education has proven fertile ground for the division of labour, and reduction in worker's autonomy. Many teachers, who see the resulting division of labour and loss of overall control as disempowering, oppose these practices. One of the reasons why many individuals have welcomed the emergence of online forms of distance education is that this is seen as once again integrating the job of the teacher, enabling him or her both to develop the web-based materials and conduct the online class discussions.

But there is some evidence that the number of online students that can be handled by one teacher is much the same as (or even less than) the number that is handled in a face-to-face class, while the volume of messaging and the time it takes to moderate classes online has increased workloads, necessitating the employment of teaching assistants and graduate students to do some of this work. Student support may be focused on the student in the home, but in many cases a network of learning or study centres is maintained, where students can come together to meet each other and advisors, to use facilities such as a library and computing and audiovisual equipment, and to take part in face-to-face tutorials. Setting up and maintaining such centres can be costly, most particularly where equipment such as computers is provided at sufficient levels to enable students to access resources easily.

Labour market practices. The practices discussed above can reduce costs significantly, particularly where they are combined with the employment of staff on short-term contracts where payment is on a per student, per hour, or per script basis. Many course developers, editors, producers, designers, and above all tutors are hired on this basis. Carried to the extreme, this can result in some open and distance learning institutions having almost no core academic staff.

Structural practices. Open and distance learning systems require a range of activities to be accomplished if they are to succeed, including the development, production and distribution of materials, the administration, teaching and examination of students, and the management of the organisation. While many institutions are organised around an integrated structure, others rely on external suppliers to fulfil some of these tasks. Thus it is not uncommon for open and distance learning institutions to work alongside media production agencies, printers, colleges and schools, etc., to provide services and facilities.

The globalisation of the sourcing of production and services has enabled open and distance learning institutions, in common with other enterprises, to locate production and service provision in one country, to serve the delivery of teaching services to students in a number of countries.

The different cost structures of distance and traditional forms of education argue for the application of different funding mechanisms to support open and distance learning, compared with traditional approaches. The much lower variable cost per student achievable in correspondence education and educational broadcast-based approaches, and the relatively high fixed investment costs in the development of learning materials, means that there is a strong argument in favour of a funding mechanism that reflects not just the number of students in the system, but the number of courses being developed and maintained.

The application of traditional per capita funding models to distance tends to underfund such institutions in the start-up phase, when large sums are required to develop the infrastructure and curriculum, and overfund them when they reach mega-institutional size, because standard per capita funding exceeds the actual level of variable costs per student in distance education. On the other hand, the use of more refined funding models can provide funding agencies with an opportunity to make savings by delaying investment in course renewal, particularly in systems where development staff are hired on short-term contracts.

There is plenty of evidence that where fee levels are disproportionately high, relative to the discretionary income of the target population, people are stopped from applying, or from progressing through a system as quickly as they might. Against this, some students will be supported by employers. The balance of funding from government, individuals, and employers, needs careful consideration given the adverse effect of underfunding on institutional quality, and of high fees on recruitment and progress. There is a strong case for mechanisms to provide assistance to those who would otherwise be denied the opportunity to study for financial reasons. Apart from fees, education generally imposes some costs on students and their families, whether it is in terms of consumables (pencils, paper), supplies (books), travel, and equipment (computers), and open and distance learning is no exception. Apart from the need to travel to study centres for face-to-face meetings, and to meet the stationery and postage costs, students may have to buy books, and equip themselves to be able to make use of the technologies used by the providers. This last may require students to own or at least have access to radios, televisions, cassette players, computers, printers, telecommunication facilities, ISP providers, etc. Most mass systems do not have the resources to provide every student with reception equipment, or even to provide sufficient facilities in study centres to enable students to use the facilities easily. The impact of technology choices on student access is an important issue —particularly in developing countries. The current push towards e-education has made the issue of access to technology even more important.

Although there are many responsible commercial providers whose standards are assured through trade organisations, there are also unscrupulous operators who maximise income by collecting non-refundable fees up-front, and minimise costs by providing minimal support to students. The practice of relying on dropout money to generate a commercial profit not only reinforces the sense of failure of weak students, but continues to give distance education a bad name, and underlines the continuing need to protect consumers against the activities of disreputable diploma mills.

Recently distance educators have come to recognise that there are very considerable differences in the nature and hence in the quality of the experience provided by interactive e-education systems, compared with earlier forms of distance education. On the whole the qualitative benefits of open and distance learning are a contentious area of debate. On the plus side, distance education students may have access to the best teaching materials, and the greatest lecturers. Student support services can also be designed to provide high quality advice and support. On the minus side, the learning materials can be seen to be pre-selected and overpackaged, and so fail to give students the chance of browsing through a library.

The major drawback in earlier forms of distance education was the lack of opportunities for dialogue and argument between teachers and students, and among students. Assuming that interactivity has been designed into the programme, it is the ability of electronic conferencing systems to get round this, and to enable students to search out materials and thus assume more responsibility for their own learning, that above anything else makes e-education attractive to distance educators, and there is some evidence that students studying online perform beyond expectations. In general, distance education liberates individuals from the tyranny of fixed-location, fixed-time education. Moreover, by virtue of its use of standardised learning materials, procedures, and processes, open and distance learning systems can easily teach very large numbers of students. It can increase the supply of places at primary, secondary, and tertiary levels of formal education, in non-formal settings, and for training, thus easing frustrated demand for entry to education. In this connection, its contribution to the provision of educational places worldwide is growing steadily. Furthermore, it can provide opportunities to people who cannot make use of traditional educational services, by meeting the needs of those in remote communities, peripatetic individuals who need to study wherever they are.

REFERENCES

Daniel, J., "Distance learning in the era of networks: What are the key technologies?" Paper presented at the Pan Commonwealth Forum on Open Learning, Brunei, 1-5 March, 1999.

Filipczak, B., "Putting the Learning into Distance Learning", *Training* 32. :111-118, October, 1995.

Keith, Harry, John Magnus, and Keegan Desmond (eds.), *Distance Education: New Perspectives,* New York: Routledge Publishers, 1993.

Keegan, D., *The Foundations of Distance Education*, London: Croom Helm, 1986.

Lockwood, Fred, ed., *Open and Distance Learning Today*, London and New York: Routledge Publishing, 1995.

Moore, M. G., and G. Kearsley, *Distance Education: A Systems View*, Belmont, Calif.: Wadsworth Publishing, 1996.

Petre, et. al., "Innovations in Large-Scale Supported Distance Teaching: Transformation for the Internet, Not Just Translation", *Journal of Engineering Education*, October 1998.

Rumble, G., *The Costs and Economics of Open and Distance Learning*, London: Kogan Page, 1997.

Taylor, J.C., "Distance education technologies: The fourth generation". *Australian Journal of Educational Technology*, 11, 2, 1-7, 2000.

8

Distance Learning Trends

Throughout the world, we are experiencing seismic shifts in how education is perceived and how it is designed, delivered and administered. These changes in education, as in other walks of life, result largely from the invention of new information and communication technologies (ICT's). Online, web-based delivery of information and interactions, seen by many as the key technological innovation of the last decade of the twentieth century, has attracted the attention of mainstream educators to the idea of distance education in a way that no earlier technology managed to do. It seems that such interest is likely to increase as the cost of bandwidth continues to fall, as the reach of the principal pipes for broad bandwidth increases, and last mile solutions such as digital subscriber lines become more prevalent.

A growing number of colleges and universities now offer some form of online distance education. For example, in the United States, over half of the 5,010 higher educational institutions offered electronically delivered distance education courses during the 1997-98 academic year. Another one-fifth of such institutions were planning to add distance education classes within the next three years. According to the National Center for Education Statistics (NCES) there were an estimated 1,661,100 enrolments in all electronically delivered distance education courses and 1,363,670 enrolments in college-level, credit-granting distance education courses, with most of these at the undergraduate level. A report issued by the International

Data Corporation (IDC) for in January 1999 titled Online Distance Learning in Higher Education, 1998-2002, estimated that 2.2 million college students will be enrolled in US distance education by 2002. IDC's research estimates that by 2002, 85 per cent of two-year colleges and 84 per cent of four year colleges will offer distance learning courses.

Traditionally in higher distance education there have been slightly more female students than male and considerably more older people than younger. In US a typical finding being that almost half of the distance students in one institution were between 31 and 46 years old. Most students are employed outside the home in one study and are domestically settled. In a 1996 study, 90 per cent of the respondents were employed and about 75 per cent were married. According to the US National Center for Educational Statistics study, of the 1,230 college-level degree programmes offered through distance education, the two main fields in which courses were offered were the general field of English, humanities, and the social and behavioural sciences and the field of business and management. The general pattern was for institutions to offer for-credit distance education courses more at the undergraduate than at the graduate/ first-professional level.

Distance education delivery systems vary enormously. Not only in the technologies they use, the numbers of students they serve, the curriculum they offer, but also in their organisational structures, governance, how they employ human resources, how they support learners, how they provide instruction, how they evaluate learning and how their learning is recognised in the world. In order to make good decisions, policy makers need to understand the strengths and weaknesses of the different types of system.

The main features of the different types of delivery systems are as follows:

i) *Mixed mode institutions:* This is the most common form of distance education in higher education. It has many similarities to traditional text-based correspondence study, with important additional features, such as learner-learner intercalation and occasional synchronous interactions. Individual students take courses delivered on the internet that are not very similar to what is taught by the same teachers in their conventional classrooms. Most of the design of instruction and the interaction with the learner is provided by the same instructor, who communicates by internet typically with about 30 students. This approach does not require significant changes in resource allocations, particularly the role of the teacher, and is widely popular for those reasons.

Distance learning programmes are often used in conventional classrooms under the control of a classroom teacher to fill curricular areas for which there may not be locally available instructors. In the US this approach has been popular in children's schools for teaching foreign languages and certain mathematics courses, with much of the instruction delivered by satellite television. Tele-courses, i.e., courses based on broadcast television has significant following. Since this approach simply enriches conventional teaching and does not require any important alteration of organisational or resource arrangements, it is non-threatening to established educational interests and generally popular among educators and policy makers who want to be seen to be embracing new technology.

ii) *Single mode DL systems*: In single mode institutions, notably the open universities in many countries, there is no activity other than the design and delivery of courses for distant learners. A significant feature of the single-mode system is the way its human resources are organised. It is no longer a matter of an individual professor teaching his course. The course is taught by the institution. It is the work of teams of specialists, media specialists, knowledge specialists, instructional design specialists, and learning specialists. Teams are more able to take advantage of the knowledge of instructional designers, which invariably leads to much higher quality course design. Due to the high investment costs, programmes delivered by single mode institutions tend to be distributed over a large population; this may require negotiation and agreements among several or many existing providers; large budgets are needed; long periods of design time are needed.

iii) *Cooperative model*: This is the most recent model of distance education. The idea is that is that a nation or region does not set up a new single mode distance education institution nor depend entirely on mixed mode types of distance education in which national resources are fragmented among the many providers. Instead, there is developed a virtual system, one that draws on the best resources wherever they are located, i.e., the content experts, instructional designers, the full range of communications technologies and all the resources needed to provide a learner support system, and configures whatever mixture is needed for a particular programme or project on a flexible, open, "mix and match" basis. Such systems need a small permanent management team of administrators and specialists in design, technology and learner support, to commission, on a contractual basis, the mixture of personnel and other resources needed for each particular project.

The permanent, experienced, management team is one key part of the system; the other is a significant funding resource. The only way the management team can obtain the quality resources needed, on a pro-term basis, guarantee quality, monitor, train, and in every way maximise the human and other resources available is by the power of funding. What this approach brings about is a very flexible, versatile, responsive system, producing high quality without commitment to ongoing institutional costs, and without the tendency to conservatism that blocs continued innovation within established educational agencies. Above all, it stimulates partnerships and employs the comparative advantage of each institution in a country or region.

iv) *University consortia*: Where the term "virtual university" is used it usually means a consortial effort by some higher education institutions to use a common technology delivery system, while maintaining independence in curriculum, instruction and management. In US, according to a 1999 survey by the State Higher Education Executive Officers (SHEEO), 33 states have created such statewide consortia or have elected to participate in a regional or national consortium. In order to improve access to library services for distance education students, almost all of the responding states offer inter-library loans, access to statewide networks, and electronic library databases. An alliance of about 50 universities, the National Technological University (NTU) provides graduate and continuing education to engineers, technical professionals, and managers worldwide. Satellite telecommunication and compressed digital video (CDV) technology link NTUs member universities to more than 1,000 work locations internationally.

v) *Corporate universities*: Many corporations have established their own corporate universities to meet the increased need for "just-in-time" and "just-enough" education. Some of these corporate universities, like Motorola University, have built physical facilities globally to meet employee-training needs while others, such as Dell University, only exist virtually and have no campuses at all. The new profit-making private sector providers are unencumbered by many of the restrictions placed on management in both public and private non-profit educational institutions. Most for-profit providers are free of the fixed costs of dormitories, classrooms, grounds, sports facilities, and many other costs other than those of direct academic, technical, and administrative support and the minimum physical infrastructure necessary to house the providers of these services.

vi) *Education companies*: Companies are being established for the purpose of selling educational services online. Examples include: Hartcourt, Hungryminds, Smartplanet, eHigher Education and large multinational for-profits such as Global Knowledge, and Suntek Information Systems, etc. Harcourt General, parent company of Harcourt Brace, is creating a for-profit university to offer courses entirely through distance education. Called Harcourt Learning Direct, the school plans to offer degree programmes in the fields of business, health care systems and administration, information technology, and general studies. The companies of eCollege and eHigherEducation have just announced a partnership to provide management and capital to colleges and universities to support their online programmes. SmartForce, another "e-learning" company, provides online mentors to its online courses, a library of laboratory simulations, threaded discussion forums on particular vendor products or generic developments in the IT industry, and the chance to interact with guest speakers on a pay-per-view basis.

Since the invention of distance education in the nineteenth century its core mission has been to open access to those who were denied opportunity in the conventional systems. This is changing. Today's developments in distance education are driven primarily by enthusiasm for technology combined with a growing view of education as a consumer commodity. As a result distance learning may no longer be narrowing the gap between those with knowledge and those who have less, but may in fact be contributing to widening it. To access the new forms of distance education requires, first, access to the new technology, and this is not equally available, a phenomenon known as the "digital divide".

In the US, where at the end of 1998 over 40 per cent of households owned computers and one-quarter of all households had internet access, high income households were 20 times more likely to have access to the internet than low income families.

Information "have-nots" are at a distinct disadvantage when it comes to taking courses online. A major barrier for the traditionally under-represented in higher education is the lack of computer or online service both in the home and in elementary and secondary schools. For instance, in US three-quarters of households with incomes over $75,000 have a computer, compared with one-third of households between $25,000 and $35,000, and one-sixth with incomes below $15,000. Regardless of income level, people living in rural areas are lagging behind those in urban areas in internet access. Indeed, at the lowest income levels, those in urban areas are more than twice as likely to have internet access than those earning the same income in rural areas

If the private sector makes the most effective use of new technologies and is able to organise the division of labour needed to increase quality while reducing costs, better than the public institutions, the profitable "low hanging fruit" will be gobbled up by the private profit-making sector. This will leave the public and private non-profit institutions to grapple with the higher-cost learners, meaning the least advantaged who need close emotional and other support as well as content areas that may be socially and personally of great value but do not give immediate returns to investment in the form of increased wages.

Since there are as yet no really large-scale providers there is little or no proof that the potential returns to scale in this approach can be realised in higher education. Research shows that the up-front costs of preparing an online course, even if done by the professor in the "mixed mode" institution, are higher than for traditional courses. The cost of interaction with students via e-mail and chat groups may also be higher. Only when the market is large and/or the interaction can be in part automated or conducted by lower cost professionals than world-class "star" professors and professional instructional designers, is cost-saving possible.

The potential decrease in unit costs—with good quality depends on reaching large markets over which to defray the higher fixed costs of course preparation and delivery, together with the substitution of high-priced labour by either lower unit cost technology or cheaper substitutes for traditional academic teaching personnel. These larger markets have not yet materialised. In fact, many universities seem to be following a policy akin to those e-commerce companies that are investing without profit or even very large numbers of "customers" in the expectation that demand will eventually catch up with supply.

Intellectual property rights are issues of copyright ownership, translated into the digital age where the cost of reproduction and transmission are virtually zero. At least two kinds of issues have arisen. The first has to do with the ownership of "courses". Are they the property of the professor or of the institution where he works? The second has to do with materials available online in digital libraries or their equivalents. In the case of course ownership, the question is more one of labour relations—the relationship of the professor to the university—which may be quite different when the professor is no longer a jack-of-all-trades, but one member of a team, the subject matter expert.

A major area of criticism is that the development of web-based learning systems will make cultural diversity one of the first victims of globalisation in distance learning and perhaps cultural decay a second. This is because of the huge potential for reaping returns to scale, and the head start that English-speaking countries have in ownership of the technology in this field. Against these forces for homogenisation and lowering standards are arrayed several opposing forces: the tenacity of cultural affiliation of many groups and countries, the just-over-the-horizon potential for high-quality automatic translation, and the trend for developing individualised instruction through the use of intelligent agents, artificial intelligence programmes, and the like. These factors together make it possible to tailor instruction to each individual's language and learning style, the latter in part culturally determined.

Another criticism is that if distance learning becomes even further a product to be bought and sold in the market, cheap but inferior educational versions will drive out good but more expensive ones. Against this one can argue that as in other markets, institutions to assess quality are likely to arise, though this has not happened so far, and that there will always be buyers ready to pay more for a superior product.

The dropout rates are higher for distance education than for face-to-face education. This may be difficult to evaluate because of the difficulty of defining a dropout in conventional education, where dropping a course and substituting another is not reported as a "dropout". However, research and experience show that there are ways to lower dropout rates, and these include developing active participation and interaction among participants in the learning process. This can be done in a variety of ways—development of study groups, joint exercises by groups of students, direct interaction at a distance between teachers and learners and the like.

If learners are alone at their computers interacting with a computer, there are a number of social skills which can be acquired in face-to-face learning environments that may be more difficult or impossible to achieve. On the other hand, research shows that students of a reflective cognitive style as compared with the impulsive, i.e., normally reserved students, are more likely to participate actively when they can think about what they want to say for some time before interacting asynchronously; and when they do not need to worry about "how they look". Facilitators can and are being hired and trained to encourage, stimulate and support online interaction between students. The issue is less serious for training people already in the labour force, assuming they are in organised work settings where face-to-face interaction is commonplace.

With the fast-growing interest in using ICTs in education, and the adoption of the terminology of distance education by those who use such technologies, the field is characterised by wide and growing conceptual confusion. This is damaging from both a practical policy makers' point of view as well as academically. As the basis for public policy, such confusion among those who gather, report and discuss distance education, sometimes means that what they study and report is the same phenomenon, but often it is not.

GLOBAL TRENDS

Considering the challenges of education and development, both in developing and developed countries, it is not surprising that open and distance learning is often seen as an important new approach and strategy which could make a significant contribution towards resolving problems of access, quality and equity. When conventional systems and approaches cannot meet the needs, it is necessary to look for new strategies. Confidence seems to be growing that open and distance learning is such a strategy. Examples of this growing confidence can be found in many countries.

For example, it has been recommended that distance education efforts in the nine high-population countries (Bangladesh, Brazil, China, Egypt, India, Indonesia, Mexico, Nigeria and Pakistan, referred to as the E-9 countries), focus on expanding work for school equivalence, for teacher education, and for non-formal education, especially in relation to health. The European Union has in recent years consistently increased distance education components of its educational programmes, and has included open and distance learning explicitly in its Maastricht Treaty. In Central and Eastern Europe, distance education is seen as an important means of supporting the transformation process towards democratic and market-oriented societies. Similar initiatives and statements are forthcoming from a wide range of individual countries as well as from regional and international organisations and agencies.

In developing countries the general lack of resources in the economy often prevents distance education programmes from being sustained, developed and extended. In addition to the general objective of increased productivity, and usually reluctant to take money away from established educational interests, governments want to have an increasing proportion of expenditure for open and distance learning to be paid by the students through fees. At the same time, in increasingly market-oriented educational systems, conventional institutions are to a greater extent using some form of open and distance learning as a means of extending their markets. Strategic alliances are being formed between educational and private sector institutions of various kinds. This means that the traditional distinctions between various types of providers are being blurred, particularly within vocational and continuing education and training.

Technological development allows for new paradigms of access and new delivery systems, linked to new types of demand. Continuous miniaturisation of equipment, reduced costs, increased user flexibility, portability and integration offer a whole range of new opportunities. These changes can either lead to more effective centralised systems of development, and the distribution of educational services and software. They can also support a more open 'networked society' with greater variation and more equitable access to educational resources through a network infrastructure.

The direction of this development will be strongly influenced by the willingness of governments to provide leadership and coordination concerning network development and access. New technology also means that distance learners are not as highly reliant on the quality of pre-produced packages of course materials or programmes as they were. Technology permits more learner-instructor and learner-learner communication and dialogue and thus a high degree of individualisation of learning and learner construction of knowledge.

Nevertheless the quality of the learning programme will depend on well designed instructional materials as well as the ability of the instructor to facilitate such knowledge construction. This puts a high premium on teachers being adequately grounded and trained in distance education methods. Finally, the trend towards internationalisation is clear. In addition to the political and economic driving forces, the internationalisation of distance education is enhanced by its links to information and communication technologies (ICTs). For instance, educational software is often international, and satellites and electronic networks allow transmission and communication across national borders. The global classroom is no longer a concept only of our imagination or of the future.

Current trends in regional development of open and distance learning system are briefly described below.

Africa

In Sub-Saharan Africa, open and distance learning has been mainly used to widen access to basic education and to maintain and improve quality in the conventional education system, particularly through in-service training of teachers. Open and distance learning has also been used in non-formal education and community development by national and international organisations. Correspondence education has been the main medium of instruction in the region, with radio also widely used. Radio transmitters reach over 60 per cent of the population whereas television coverage is usually confined to major towns. Interactive technologies have been of limited value in a region in which the availability of telephone lines is about five times lower than the average low-income country and where the telephones are concentrated in urban, relatively privileged, areas.

In the past it seems that open and distance learning has had a relatively low impact on education in the region. The main reasons concern not only lack of infrastructure, but also include underfunding, lack of training of those involved, as well as the fragmented institutional base which results in both duplication of programmes and insufficient concentration of the limited resources on any one. The situation seems to have improved over the past five years, with evidence of growing commitment by African governments to the development of ICTs along with interest in the application of those technologies for distance education.

Today, there are strong indicators that open and distance learning is becoming more central to the education policy of many countries. Among examples from particular countries can be cited South Africa's Technology Enhanced Learning Programme and its Telematics for African Development Consortium. In South Africa, projects such as the Shoma teacher development programme using satellite TV and internet technology to support in-service training for underqualified teachers demonstrate the potential of partnerships between private companies and national and provincial departments of education. A remarkable phenomenon in South Africa in the early years of the new decade is the shift on the part of learners from single mode to dual mode institutions.

In Botswana, the major distance education provider is the Botswana College of Distance and Open Learning (BOCODOL). BOCODOL currently offers distance education courses for the Junior Certificate which is the end of basic education, and which constitutes the first 10 years of formal schooling. It also offers distance education courses for the General Certificate in Secondary Education (GCSE). It is being given a brief to continue offering school equivalence programmes and additional vocational and non-formal courses for both adults and youth. It uses printed materials, which are distributed in the post and regional offices as study centres for students to meet tutors.

Malawi has two dedicated distance education providers, one a private school and the other a department of the Ministry of Education, Sports and Culture. The University of Malawi has been exploring possibilities for offering distance education programmes, and the Domasi College of Education has taken the initiative to adopt distance learning as an approach to the training of teachers. The College has collaborated with the Commonwealth of Learning and is developing modules for this purpose. MIITEP, an in-service programme run by the Teacher Development Unit to train untrained and underqualified teachers, employs open and distance learning methods for delivery of the programme. In addition, the newly established Mzuzu University is also planning to offer teacher education courses through distance education.

In Tanzania, distance education is organised through the Distance Education Association of Tanzania (DEATA). Its membership is currently made up of the Ministry of Education and Culture, the Open University of Tanzania, the University of Dar-es-Salaam, the Vocational Education and Training Authority, the Muhimbili University College for Health Sciences, the Southern African Extension Unit, the Institute of Adult Education, and the Cooperative College Moshi. These organisations enrol over 18,000 students between them.

In Zimbabwe, the Centre for Distance Education was established by the University of Zimbabwe in 1993 and in 1996 became the University College of Distance Education. The college received its university charter in 1999, and was transformed into a fully-fledged university known as the Zimbabwe Open University. Among other things, the university's mission is to adapt, develop, and implement new courses and programmes to meet the needs of a changing knowledge base, employment sector, and socioeconomic, political, and international environment.

In Africa, there are many initiatives to establish networking through national and regional associations in order to strengthen and improve capacities for open and distance learning in the region. The projects that exemplify this collaborative approach include training of upper primary and junior secondary science, technology and mathematics teachers in Africa by distance; training for primary school principals, using print materials and internet, coordinated by the International Francophone Consortium of Distance and Open Learning Institutions (CIFFAD), etc.

Arab States

In Arab states open and distance education is generally more recent and less extensive. However, there is a growing interest in the potential of distance education to solve some of the educational challenges facing the region.

Although Egypt reports using communication technologies in school and both radio and video-conferencing for teacher education, the level of usage of distance education is lower than in other E-9 countries.

In Algeria, the Centre National d'Enseignement Generalise offers general and technical education to Baccalaureate level, education in preparation for certificates and diplomas of different levels, and specialist professional training.

Since 1984, the Sudan Open Learning Organisation (SOLO) has operated to provide a number of educational programmes including basic education to adult refugees in Ethiopia, Somalia and Sudan. At the basic level it offers a literacy programme, a primary health care programme, income generating and small business skills for women, and a teacher assistance course aimed at training basic level teachers employed within the refugee schools.

The Palestinian Al-Quds Open University began teaching in 1991, at the higher education level, using an integrated multimedia approach. Set up to meet the needs of Palestinian students in Gaza and the West Bank, the University initially operating out of Amman, moved its headquarters to Jerusalem in 1993.

Recently, the Arab Open University project has been formally established with its headquarters in Kuwait. Plans are afoot to launch programmes in a number of Arab countries (Bahrain, Egypt, Jordan, Kuwait, Lebanon and Saudi Arabia), with others to follow. Meanwhile, the level of frustrated demand for entry to higher education has attracted foreign providers to the region.

Pacific

Australia's open and distance learning dates back to the first decade of the nineteenth century, giving the system long experience from which significant lessons have been drawn by later open and distance learning initiatives. Dual mode institutions characterise open and distance learning in Australia, providing similar curriculum for on- and off-campus students. This promotes student choice and flexibility combining courses in a variety of modes in accordance with student needs.

Australia's open and distance learning provision aims to improve access and outcomes for disadvantaged and disenfranchised populations, including the aboriginal peoples and Torres Strait Islanders. However, current threats from competitive global markets, especially with growing virtual/online learning, are demanding the adoption of more flexible and commercial approaches. The Australian open and distance learning providers are well-equipped with high level technologies. Asynchronous rather than synchronous forms of learning have been adopted in order to promote flexibility for the learner.

South Pacific

Open and distance learning in island nations of South Pacific region is offered at several institutions including the University of the South Pacific (USP), the University of Papua New Guinea

(UPNG), the University of Technology in Papua New Guinea, Fiji School of Medicine, Fiji School of Nursing, the Solomon Islands College of Higher Education, Pacific Adventist College in Papua New Guinea, the Pacific Theological College of Fiji, the Fiji College of Advanced Education and Tonga Teachers College and the Community Training Center in Tonga. Established in 1968 as a regional university the University of the South Pacific (USP) developed into a dual mode institution in 1970, with a main campus in Fiji and smaller campuses at Vanuatu and Samoa. The university maintains a centre in all 12 member countries.

Currently about 5,000 students in the region are enrolled in open and distance learning provision, with the target to increase that enrolment by 10 per cent per year. Courses offered are equivalent to those on campus and follow the same semester system. English remains the language of instruction. Constrained by communication and geographical barriers, open and distance learning in the region has relied on correspondence programmes and occasional face-to-face tutorials.

South-east Asia

In China, open and distance learning has significantly contributed to broadening access and opportunities especially to higher education and to socioeconomic development more generally. China's open and distance learning focuses on secondary and tertiary education, although programmes for in-service adult education and training are also offered. Generally the media include correspondence, television and radio broadcasts, and State Examination Self-Study (SESS). With the establishment of the Radio and TV University system (RTVU) in 1960, China became the first country to use radio and television to provide single mode distance higher education with unified planning. Today its single mode distance RTVUs makes up one of the 11 world mega-universities.

Hong Kong has only one distance education university, the Open University of Hong Kong (OUHK), but the provision of open and distance learning also comes from other countries. Thus there are two categories of open and distance learning programmes, local and off-shore. The off-shore programmes are provided from different countries including: Britain (288 courses or 57 per cent of the programmes), Australia (157 courses or 31 per cent), US (7 per cent), and mainland China (4 per cent). Canada, Macau and Ireland provide the rest. Partnerships with local institutions have been sought, although local partners contribute little to the content of the programmes.

In Indonesia open and distance learning had its beginnings in 1955 with the establishment of correspondence diploma programmes. In 1981 open and distance learning programmes became widespread with the introduction of a crash teacher-training programme. The University of Terbuka (UT), the Indonesian Open Learning University, was established in 1984 and remains the only single mode distance education university in the country. UT aims at providing flexible inexpensive education, reaching people unable to attend face-to-face education, increasing access to higher education, providing training in areas demanded by economic and cultural development, and upgrading the qualifications of primary and secondary school teachers.

The credibility of distance education in Indonesia is reflected in the increasing numbers of enrolments at UT, the establishment of distance education programmes in other institutions, and the establishment of the Indonesian Distance Learning Network (IDLN) by 13 institutions to share training, research and information. With its headquarters in Jakarta, supported by 13 regional offices, UT uses both centralised and decentralised management approaches and collaborates with external institutions such as the national postal services, Bank Rakyat Indonesia, and provincial governments.

Print materials developed by course teams remain the main medium of instruction while conventional examinations, self-tests, course practicums and micro-teaching make up the basis of student assessment.

In Japan, until 1985 there were only a few private correspondence colleges and the University of the Air (UA). By 2000 there were 19 four-year open and distance learning private universities and 10 junior colleges with an enrolment of over 254,000 students. Four of the open and distance learning universities, including UA, are planning to initiate postgraduate programmes soon. Enrolment to open and distance learning programmes in universities is determined by entry examination. Despite the fact that 99 per cent of higher institutions are 'wired', only 10 per cent fully utilise ICTs for delivery of open and distance learning. Barriers to the use of ICTs include high installation and maintenance costs, the lack of organisational support, and experience and human resource issues.

In Malaysia, open and distance learning, which is regarded as more flexible and cost-effective, has increasingly been acknowledged as a desirable alternative. Universiti Sain Malaysia (USM) began open and distance learning programmes in 1971. The challenges of the 1990s, and in particular the need to cope with economic and technological change, led Malaysia to move substantially more into open and distance learning. The country's economic down-turn in the 1990s made it more difficult for many Malaysians to afford education, especially in foreign institutions where many had previously enrolled.

For Malaysia open and distance learning provides the basis of hope that the country can achieve its goal of democratising higher education, making it accessible to the majority of the people. Currently all except two of the eleven Malaysian universities offer open and distance learning programmes. The government as well as enhancing institutional autonomy encourages the universities to adapt corporate-style management practices, deeming both important for dynamic operation and quality. The open and distance learning delivery mode in Malaysia remains mostly printed lectures supplemented by face-to-face, audio, and videocassettes. Institutions with open and distance learning programmes enrol students from all the 14 states of Malaysia and a good number from other countries including: Indonesia, Thailand, Singapore, China, and Korea.

In the Philippines open and distance learning was initiated by the US-based International Correspondence Schools (ICS) programmes in 1940. Due to the existence of many traditional tertiary institutions and the view that open and distance learning was inferior, its popularity remained low until the 1990s when the growing use of ICTs improved the image and prospects of open and distance learning worldwide. By 1995 several institutions were offering open and distance learning programmes, including the government-owned consortium (Continuing Science Education for Teachers), the Philippine Women's University (PWU), University of Mindanao (UM), University of the Philippines Los Banos (UPLB), the Polytechnic University of the Philippines (PUP), and the Visayas State College of Agriculture (ViSCA).

Currently prospects for open and distance learning, including the possibility of government funding, have attracted more colleges and universities to initiate open and distance learning programmes. However, the lack of open and distance learning experience has led to haphasardly managed and delivered open and distance learning programmes. This has led to the promulgation of new policies and guidelines in order to eliminate abuse of the system and to enhance quality in all open and distance learning institutions. More people and institutions are becoming connected to the internet, raising the prospects for internet-based education. Currently, however, printed material, radio, television and occasional face-to-face remain dominant.

In Thailand open and distance learning began in 1933 with the establishment of the University of Moral and Political

Science. By the year 2000 more open and distance learning institutions have emerged including Ramkhamhaeng University (RU), Sukhothai Thammathirat Open University (STOU), the Department of Non-Formal Education (DNFE), Klai Kangwon Royal Satellite Project (KKRSP), the Borderless Education Project (BEP) and Suranaree University of Technology (SUT). In collaboration with international agencies all open and distance learning programmes are provided nationwide, are self-funded and, depending on the institution and programme pursued, one may study at home, on campus or a mixture of the two.

Given Thailand's comprehensive communications infrastructure, its open and distance learning utilises current technologies for instructional delivery. Most open and distance learning institutions have a multimedia instructional delivery system and the existence of internet systems has made it possible for institutions like SUT to use on-screen interactive and web-based internet media as core instructional delivery systems supplemented by print, audiovisual media and telecommunications.

Most open and distance learning programmes are in the area of social sciences, except for those offered at STOU and the planned technology-based programmes offered at BEP beginning in 2002. Recognising open and distance learning's potential for cost-effectiveness, mass enrolment, and the provision of education and training without demanding the movement of employees, Thailand currently considers open and distance learning as a most economical and effective way to educate and train.

South Asia

In India open and distance learning started in the 1960s. By the 1980s there were 34 universities offering correspondence education through departments designed for that purpose. The first single mode open university was established in Andhra

Pradesh in 1982, followed by the Indira Gandhi National Open University (IGNOU), and subsequently in Bihar, Rajasthan, and Maharashtra, Madhya Pradesh, Gujarat, Karnataka, West Bengal, and Uttar Pradesh. The establishment of these single mode distance education universities was stimulated by the government's intention to democratise education and make it lifelong. The initiative did not discourage the expansion at the same time of correspondence programmes in dual mode universities.

Most open and distance learning universities in India co-ordinate communication and collaboration through the Distance Education Council (DEC), founded in 1992. DEC is responsible for the promotion, coordination, and the maintenance of quality and standards. A range of factors including emerging ICTs, liberalisation, privatisation and globalisation have amplified the demand for open and distance learning. While the government is responsible for more than 90 per cent of open and distance learning funding, plans are underway to involve the private sector more closely, especially through permitting the increase of fees.

In Bangladesh the Education Reform Commission (1957) recommended the establishment of a correspondence school. This led to the establishment of the East Pakistan Audiovisual Education Center (AVEC) in 1962 and the School Broadcasting Programme (SBP) in 1980. AVEC and SBP merged into the National Institute of Educational Media and Technology (NIEMT) that later became the Bangladesh Institute of Distance Education (BIDE).

Successes with BIDE provided the impetus for the establishment of the Bangladesh Open University (BOU). BOU has more than 200,000 students enrolled across the country, and offers diploma and degree level certificates and non-formal and informal education programmes. BOU's curriculum covers secondary and higher secondary certificate, agriculture and livestock science, teacher training, humanities, languages, business management, science and technology, non-formal and informal programmes. With the goal to use limited computer- and internet-based communication in the near future, BOU's core instructional delivery media remain printed materials, radio and television broadcast, occasional face-to-face, and limited teleconferencing.

Europe

In European countries open and distance learning is well-established, even though the status and tradition varies considerably within the region. In Western Europe there is a strong private sector serving the adult population, mainly through general education programmes at the secondary level, through various forms of vocational and professional training and through non-formal education. A number of countries have implemented particular legislative measures to ensure quality control of private provision. Some countries have also established major government-funded institutions. Some of these operate mainly at the secondary level, others also have tertiary level programmes.

The UK Open University has set the standards for a particular type of university institution, the open universities. Flagship institutions have been established in other European countries including most notably Spain with the Universidad Nacional de Educación a Distancia (UNED) and the Universitat Oberta de Catalunya (UoC), Germany with the Fernuniversität, as well as the Open Universiteit of the Netherlands and the Universidade Aberta of Portugal. In other countries the dual mode type of universities represent the dominant model, and in recent years various consortia models have been introduced, including virtual and distributed universities.

European distance education is currently at a stage of major strategic development, where national provision is being extended across borders. In Central and Eastern Europe and the former USSR the political and economic transformations have had important implications for education, and have already led to fundamental reforms and restructuring of national education systems. In most of the countries, distance education based on correspondence studies combined with face-to-face consultations was developed and served large populations. However, student numbers decreased very much after the political transformation, partly due to lack of support from employers. The model is now often met with some reserve regarding both status and quality.

Open and distance learning is still a priority for most of the governments in Central and Eastern Europe but it is in need of fundamental reform and upgrading, as is the education system as a whole. The development of new structures will need support in forms of funding and regional collaboration in order to be effective, such as the PHARE and TACIT Programmes of the European Commission.

The European Union is promoting distance education, particularly with a European dimension and in cooperation between institutions in the member states. Open and distance learning features strongly in policy documents from the Commission of the European Communities, and was mentioned particularly in the 1992 Maastricht Treaty. Support for distance education is also given within the framework of programmes of economic assistance to Central and Eastern Europe and the former USSR. This continuous interest of the European Union has probably influenced national governments in their revision of policy concerning open and distance learning.

Several regional networks have been formed since the second half of the 1980s, among them the European Distance Education Network (EDEN), and the European Association of Distance Teaching Universities (EADTU). They are active in promoting and implementing collaborative projects in various sectors and at different levels.

Substantial progress in the quality of supply of multimedia products and services for education and training has taken place over the recent period. The explosion of internet use and the significant growth of the CD-ROM market represent the two basic conditions for this development on the technology infrastructure side. The quality of multimedia products has improved substantially, moving from an unsatisfactory level which justified negative attitudes developed in the past by users and intermediaries.

New forms of user-based review are emerging in some countries. High growth has taken place in the diffusion of ICTs in all European countries, and the trend is expected to continue vigorously, especially in those countries that are less advanced. Education and training is responsible for about one-third of multimedia development. A sort of virtuous circle is created, in which users familiarise themselves with multimedia tools in the context of entertainment activities, and then become able and willing to use multimedia products and services either for education or for training purposes.

Public authorities in the main European countries have understood the significance of educational multimedia and the number of initiatives at the local, national and European levels has multiplied. They are taking shape through the setting up of financial support funds, and incentives to develop infrastructures and programmes, and through lowering the costs of equipment for schools. A potentially significant new fact is the emergence of multi-country projects directly supported by national Ministries of Education, which have among their objectives to involve private partnerships in a systematic way.

Diversity and fragmentation in Europe goes beyond the structure and traditions of the education system. Severe obstacles for development include lack of standardisation, varying and insufficient copyright legislation and weaknesses in the European software industry. Proper regulatory frameworks, tariff structures and the seamless interconnection of networks, as well as the development of services and applications, are crucial for further utilisation of new technologies. The European Union has carried out actions in this area, including open and distance learning, based on recommendations from a group chaired by Commissioner

Martin Bangemann. This has been extended most recently with the e-Learning Action Plan, and the extension of opportunities to develop open and distance learning activities for countries using the European Commission Framework Programmes.

Latin America and the Caribbean

Early provision of distance education in Latin America dates from 1946 and the establishment of Radio Sutatenza by Accion Communitaria Popular. The programme which presaged the development of the Latin American radio-phonic school model delivered correspondence and radio-based education to adults.

Radio schools, generally supported by government and the Roman Catholic Church, were set up in almost all the countries of the region and played an important role in rural community education and development, and in the provision of school-equivalency programmes. One particularly successful project was Accion Cultural Popular (ACPO), which operated from 1974 to 1998, and which used educational radio supported by books, pamphlets and charts to provide Colombian peasants and their children with basic literacy and numeracy skills, as well as community development, health education, child care and agricultural skills. ACPO died after 40 years when church and government support was withdrawn.

In Bolivia Radio San Gabriel offers a range of basic education programmes to adult Aymarans, with a view to helping these people integrate themselves more fully into Bolivian life.

In Brazil, the Centro de Ensino Tecnologico de Brasilia offers basic education. The Centros APEC de Ensenanza a Distancia in the Dominican Republic, with some 22,000 students each year, offer upper primary and lower secondary level courses, as well as vocational and skills courses in such topics as Small Business Management and Home Electrical Installation. Project ACESSO in Brazil is a comparatively rare example of a vocationally-oriented project that offers basic education components to its target group—the workers of PETROBRAS, the Brazilian state-owned oil company.

In Chile the Instituto Nacional de Capacitacion Profesional established a distance education programme in 1975 to offer further education and vocational courses, basic occupational training, and technological training at a distance.

In-school educational television (ETV), designed to deliver mass education developed in the 1960s and were applied in Brazil, Colombia, El Salvador, and Mexico. They were invariably aimed at children. In some cases, as in El Salvador and Mexico, they demonstrated the ability to improve the quality of the educational process and outcome, but they were generally too costly to sustain and by the mid-1980s many of the schemes had been wound up.

The Mexican Telesecundaria is an exception. Well integrated into national provision, it provides middle school opportunities to people in rural communities, attracting the poorer and more remote students. In 2000/2001 it had over 963,000 students in some 50,000 groups spread over 16,000 schools, had 23,000 students enrolled in Costa Rica, the Dominican Republic, El Salvador, Guatemala, Honduras, and Panama, and was due to start operating in the Andean region. At primary level, Edusat (Educational Satellite Television Network), which was launched in 1995, reaches over 10,000 schools throughout Mexico to provide basic education to remote, outlying regions.

Brazil's Telecurso has been running since the 1960s and recently launched a new programme of basic education for young adults, which now reaches 200,000 students. A further 200,000 students attend classes in regular schools that rely on Telecurso programmes.

In Latin American countries, schools radio broadcasting and Interactive Radio Instruction (IRI) concerned with improving the quality of learning and teaching within the classroom are spreadeded widely. IRI was first used in Nicaragua from 1974 to 1979 in the Radio Mathematics project. Although IRI projects have had mixed results in terms of national implementation and long-term sustainability, there are examples of interesting projects in mathematics in Bolivia and Venezuela, and IRI has also been applied in the Dominican Republic to provide the first four years of primary school outside formal schools. The IRI-based Preventive Health programme (PARI) in Bolivia has achieved significant gains in children's knowledge, attitudes and behaviours.

TV Escola is a Brazilian schools television service of the Secretary of Distance Education of the Ministry of Education. Some of the air-time is used for the in-service training of teachers and principals; the rest is used for programmes to support classroom teaching. Each programme lasts three hours and is re-transmitted four times per day. Started in September 1995, the project now reaches all Brazilian states. Any school with more than 100 elementary students is eligible to apply for resources from the National Fund for the Development of Education (FNDE) to buy the 'technological kit' needed to download and record the programmes delivered through the Brasilsat satellite.

During 1970s, universities in Latin America were began to set up distance education departments to reach out to marginalised populations. The Universidad de La Sabana in Colombia, for example, began offering distance courses in 1975. Some of these programmes are designed to prepare students for university. The Pre-University Programme run by the Institute of Distance and Continuing Education of the University of Guyana offers remedial programmes in English and mathematics. Others are designed to offer university-level qualifications at a distance. The predominant pattern is the dual mode university, with very many universities offering distance education programmes.

In Jamaica, the University of the West Indies Distance Teaching Experiment began regular programmes in 1983/1984, using telephone-based systems to enable courses to be taught through a combination of correspondence techniques and teleconferences, with occasional audio- and video-tapes and face-to-face sessions. In 1992 the University officially became a dual mode institution and began to offer a number of certificate and degree programmes at a distance. It provides distance education opportunities across the 14 countries served by the University.

In 1989 the Monterrey Institute of Technology and Higher Education (ITESM), Mexico, launched a virtual university to provide both within and outside Mexico a comprehensive postgraduate teaching-learning system using advanced telecommunications technologies and electronic networks.

Latin America's first two distance teaching universities—the Universidad Estatal a Distancia in Costa Rica, and the Universidad Nacional Abierta in Venezuela—were founded in 1977, to respond to strong demands for higher education, and to provide avenues by which adults could re-enter the education system. Further distance teaching universities followed, in Colombia (Universidad Nacional de Educacion a Distancia), Mexico (Sistema de Universidad Abierta), and Chile (Universidad Gran Mariscal Sucre).

In Brazil, the PROFORMACAO project provides initial training to unqualified teachers already teaching pre-school literacy, and the first four years of basic education in the state and municipal education systems. In 1977 Latin America's first two distance teaching universities, training, which takes place over 3200 hours, consists of a distance education system combining self-study course materials and school-based practice, linked to biweekly workshops.

North America

In North America distance education has a history goes back more than 100 years and is now firmly rooted in the education systems of both Canada and the USA. There is a rich variety of programmes and institutions in a range of areas, and there are examples of the use of almost every conceivable technology. In this region distance education is used for outreach to remote population groups, support of school education, provision of education and training opportunities for adults, vocational courses, corporate and military training, higher and continuing education, life enrichment courses, etc. Modalities in frequent use are web-based instruction, computer-mediated communication, video teleconferencing, satellite transmission, television and video courses, and correspondence education often supplemented by the use of CD-ROMs and videotapes.

In North American countries education is under the responsibility of individual states/provinces. There is variation in the extent to which states/provinces provide resources and infrastructure to support access to instructional opportunities and resources at a distance. A number of states and provinces have major initiatives to help schools acquire videoconferencing systems to share courses and to provide internet access in the classroom. These efforts in the USA have received support through the national E-Rate programme that provides substantial discounts to schools for telecommunications and technology access. Another USA national initiative is targeted on training teachers to use technology. The Preparing Tomorrow's Teachers to Use Technology programme has helped hundreds of colleges of education across the USA prepare teachers to use the new technologies for learning.

North American witnessed an explosive growth in the number of undergraduate and graduate courses with the advent of world wide web. In addition to offerings by 'bricks and mortar' universities, a number of for-profit online university companies and others have arisen, been accredited and are now offering web-based degree programmes. The use of traditional educational television services and videoconferencing services is continuing but is increasingly coupled with web-based resources and collaboration.

In USA, conventional universities, private distance teaching institutions, military training institutions, broadcasting services, private corporations, and a range of various consortia are among the prominent providers of distance education. In Canada, there are some strong provincial institutions at the secondary as well as university level, and also educational television services. There are, for instance, specialised distance teaching universities in Quebec, Alberta and British Columbia.

The region is having extensive experience in the application of advanced telecommunication technologies in distance education than most other parts of the world. A significant trend is that of blended distance learning programmes and systems that represent a mix of technologies such as educational television, videoconferencing, web-based communication and collaboration, and CD-ROM instructional resources. Access to the internet is available to a majority of the population at home, school, or at work, and governments see a future in expanding capacity and access through the web.

There are four long-term trends in American higher distance education that have been prophetic of the changes observed in distance education within North America and globally. They are:

i) simultaneous diversification and convergence of technologies, with consequences for course design, curriculum planning, organisation of resource investment policies, etc.;
ii) changing relationships with students with more weight on group and student-student interaction, shift of control over time, place and pace of study;
iii) changing relationships between institutions, with the development of consortia for sharing resources, provision of national degrees and programmes, and even specialised national universities or university programmes;
iv) emerging mainstream, meaning that distance education is a symptom of broader changes in the educational paradigm, where educational institutions are adapting to currents of social change, new technological infrastructures and shifts in basic teaching-learning relationships.

The new information and communication technologies have served as a catalyst for forging new partnerships between higher education institutions. The agreement on economic cooperation between North American countries in NAFTA also includes increased cooperation in distance education between Canada, USA and Mexico. Such collaborations will help to increase the quality of distance education programmes.

CHANGING LABOUR MARKET: RETHINKING EDUCATIONAL GOVERNANCE

Online education makes possible remote access to enormous databases and textbases, remote collaboration, linkage of a critical mass of learners for specialised topics, interactive conferencing and even videoconferencing, expert system-based feedback, computer simulation, multimedia, and more. While it is true that almost everything about learner-centred education could be done through manual methods, computers bring the costs in resources and time down to a level that at least the more affluent colleges and individuals may afford.

Proponents of distance education are well aware that something essential is lost when face-to-face interaction is given up in favour of computer-mediated instruction or that which comes via correspondence courses. However, they argue that this can be made up by online discussions and videoconferencing. It is easy to lose sight of the fact that online discussions and videoconferences face much the same constraints as traditional education.

If distance education incurs the added costs of courseware development yet one still has to have the same faculty size, the economic imperative of alternative delivery is undermined. Computer-based learners are: comfortable writing, are able to motivate themselves to complete assignments, and have the requisite equipment and connectivity. Developing materials requires time and expertise in pedagogy not often available to university professors who specialise in non-education courses.

Indeed, the erosion of mentoring is common in online education as face-to-face contact between student and professor is replaced by the colder and more formal computer interface and typed word. At the same time, the student is apt to suffer a diminishing of peer learning and student role modelling as well. This problem is not intrinsic to distance education, but it is endemic.

Education is narrowed toward training. Tremendous pressure is created to "teach to the test", which is what the assessment instrument in effect becomes. When distance education is part of a cost reduction effort, requiring human resources to be stretched to cover more credit hours, faculty resignation to the training mentality of outcome-based evaluation is all but assured.

Several studies have been made of the cost functions for large distance learning systems as compared with conventional institutions. Also, since staff costs are an important part of the educational budget in conventional systems, courses in this mode have a much higher cost at the university level than at the primary or secondary school levels. Distance education costs will vary less over this range so cost savings will appear greater at the higher academic levels, as evidenced by analyses from Korea, Israel, Mauritius, Kenya and Brazil. Numbers of students therefore need to be larger in the school level to maintain a similar level of cost-effectiveness.

Another issue concerns the different profile of the whole integrated distance learning system. Analyses have been undertaken which show the following features. The growing fascination with distance learning, notwithstanding the number of valid criticisms thereof, has been reinforced by a more receptive international policy environment that was the outcome of UNESCO's Education-for-All programme, along with the Delors Report of the European Commission. Both initiatives took the 1948 Universal Declaration of Human Rights and expanded its scope, noting that "every person—child, youth and adult—shall be able to benefit from educational opportunities designed to meet their basic learning needs." It was also in the 1990s that the philosophy of "lifelong learning" was introduced, as a means of preparing people for a world of accelerating change.

Understanding the impact of liberalisation upon the labour market in mainstream economic theory is primarily about recognising the importance of mobility—that is to say, the ability of an economy to transfer its labour resources from inefficient sectors, which "lose" from the liberalisation process, toward efficient sectors. The act of opening up a sector may therefore be construed as an income-redistribution policy and creates "winners" and "losers", with the magnitude of the gains and losses depending almost entirely upon the mobility of the potential losers.

In a "frictionless" economy, no one need lose from liberalisation. As it is, however, factors of production such as unskilled labour tend to be immobile or "specific", at least within the formal sector of the economy. The appropriate response to globalisation for those who believe it to be beneficial and inevitable, therefore, is to take steps to increase the mobility of specific factors—a task which many commentators would willingly assign to the state, given that mobility has strong public good characteristics.

The result of this general consensus has been a preference for safety nets with, say, a larger re-training component than those with a higher proportion of transfers. This domestic process of redistribution, however, takes place within the wider context of a so-called "international division of labour" in which technology-intensive industries locate in the developed world while progressively more labour-intensive ones move to the developing world, following direction of least-cost labour.

Most of the world's trade and investment takes place within them. Typically, the development strategies of these countries consist of some form of rural industrialisation. Among some two dozen aspiring nations, China, Thailand, Indonesia and Malaysia appear to have the best chances, but global economic conditions are now said to be less favourable than in the boom years when the Asian tigers achieved their very rapid structural transformations.

The emergence of China and Vietnam as centres of labour-intensive manufacturing in the region have put a damper on the country's hopes of developing via the traditional strategy of expanding industries requiring mass unskilled labour. Clearly there is a need to consider a different approach to industrialisation.

In developing countries, ODL helping to overcome longstanding problems of equity and access is overwhelming. In Andhra Pradesh, India, there is a programme to place working children in schools. In April 1997, the Andhra Pradesh Social Welfare Department initiated a pilot back-to-school programme for all 23 districts in the state, in which hostels operated by the department are converted into "camp schools" for two months each year. The programme identifies and enrols children who never enrolled in school or dropped out early. Special emphasis is placed on bonded children, children working as domestic servants, and children from lower castes, tribes and other socially disadvantaged backgrounds. Each hostel has approximately 100 students and five teachers. Children attend class for an average of six hours a day—the approach is modular and uses print materials produced centrally. In its initial phase in 1997, the programme enrolled 37, 000 children in schools; the Social Welfare Department plans to enrol 100, 000 students each year in the future. About 74 per cent of the students enrolled in the camps were subsequently admitted to formal schools.

The National Open School in India offers free choices from among a wide range of both academic and vocational courses to students who frequently opt for different combinations of the two areas. In addition, it offers courses for life enrichment and bridging courses at the entry level. It caters to students of all ages over 14 and has succeeded to attract women to the extent that they make up 38 per cent of its enrolment. Marginalised groups in general, including women, comprise over 50 per cent of its enrolment.

In making use of the different media, it puts great emphasis on quality aspects of the technology of text, but does not shy away from more advanced technologies, such as instructional television as well as audio and video programmes for enrichment purposes, in addition to face-to-face contact with students. By making use of the existing school network to serve its students, it benefits from that infrastructure at the same time that it enriches it by bringing in facilities not normally available to the schools. On the other hand, in-service training (INSET) programmes may then be research-based and would in principle be more supportive of efforts toward decentralisation.

REFERENCES

Bradley J. and C.Yates (eds.), *Basic Education at a Distance, World Review of Distance Education and Learning*, London: Routledge, 2000.

Euler M., and D.Von Berg, *The Use of Electronic Media in Open Learning and Distance Education*, Paris: UNESCO, 1998.

Foks, J., *Open Learning and Distance Education in South Africa: Communications for Learning*, University of Pretoria: Bureau for Academic Support Services, 1995.

Holloway, R.E., and J., Ohler, "Distance education in the next decade", In G.J. Anglin (ed.), *Instructional technology, Past, Present, and Future,* Englewood, CO: Libraries Unlimited, 1991, pp. 259-66.

Kennedy, Paul, *Preparing for the 21 st Century*, Random House, 1993.

Lockwood, Fred, ed., *Open and Distance Learning Today*, London and New York: Routledge Publishing, 1995.

UNESCO, "Learning: the Treasure Within", Report to UNESCO of the International Commission on Education for the Twenty-first Century, Paris: UNESCO, 1996.

____________, *Distance Education in the E-9 Countries, The Development and Future of Distance Education Programmes in the Nine High-Population Countries*, Paris: UNESCO, 2001.

Bibliography

Arnsten R. and A. Sheddick, Accessing Experiential Learning through Collaborative Multimedia Learning Processes, ICEL Conference, Cape town, S. Africa, July, 1996.

Bang J., H.P. Baumeister and K.Wilson, *"Collaboration as a Challenge, New Learning Environments embedded in old Traditions", in* Proceedings from EUNIS'99, Information Technology Shaping European Universities, Helsinki, 1999.

Barron, A., and G. Orwig, New Technologies for Education, Englewood, CO: Libraries Unlimited, 1993.

Barron, A., K. S. Ivers and L. Sherry, *"Exploring the Internet"*, The Computing Teacher, 22(2), 14-19, 1994.

Bates A.W., Technology, Open Learning and Distance Education, London: Routledge, 1995.

Bates, Tony, *"The Continuing Evolution of ICT Capacity: The Implications for Education" In Farrell, Glen, (ed.),* The Changing Face of Virtual Education. London: The Commonwealth of Learning, 2001, p. 29- 46.

Belanger, F. and D.H. Jordan, Evaluation and Implementation of Distance Learning: Technologies, Tools, and Techniques, Hershey, Pa.: dea Group Publishing, 2000.

Bonamy, J., B. Charlier, and M., Saunders, *'Bridging Tools' for change: evaluating a collaborative learning network.* Journal of Computer Assisted Learning, Vol. 17 (3) 295-305, 2001.

Boshier, R., M. Wilson, and A., Qayyum, *"Lifelong education and the World Wide Web: American hegemony or diverse utopia?"* International Journal of Lifelong Education, Vo.l 18 (4) 275-285, 1999.

Bradley J. and C.Yates (eds.), Basic Education at a Distance, World Review of Distance Education and Learning, London: Routledge, 2000.

Capper, Joanne, *"E-Learning Growth and Promise for the Developing World"*, TechKnowLogia, May/June, 2001, p. 7-10.

Cooper, Mark N., Disconnected, Disadvantaged, and Disenfranchised: Explorations in the Digital Divide, Washington, D.C.: Consumer Federation of American and Consumers Union, 2000.

Cowham T., 'Information and Learning Technology: A Development Handbook' in FE Matters, February, 1997.

Dalit, Jessica, *"The Policy Context of Open and Distance Learning"*, Journal of Open and Distance Learning, PUP 2000.

Daniel, J., "Distance learning in the era of networks: What are the key technologies?" Paper presented at the Pan Commonwealth Forum on Open Learning, Brunei, 1-5 March, 1999.

Dock, A. and J. Helwig (eds.), *"Interactive Radio Instruction: Impact, Sustainability and Future Directions"*, Educational Training Technology Notes, Series 4, Washington D.C., USAID/World Bank, 1999.

Dodd, T. and J. K. Mayo, "The Promise and Performance of Distance Education in Developing Nations: The IEC experience 1971-1992", Paper presented at International Extension College's Anniversary Conference, Robinson College Cambridge UK, September 1992.

Eager M., *"Distance education: The indicators"*, People Dynamics, 13(2), January, pp. 17-20, 1996.

Ellsworth, J.H., Education on the Internet, *Indianapol*is: Sams Publishing, 1994.

Euler M., and D. Von Berg, The Use of Electronic Media in Open Learning and Distance Education, Paris: UNESCO, 1998.

Euler M., and D.Von Berg, The Use of Electronic Media in Open Learning and Distance Education, Paris: UNESCO, 1998.

Evans, T. and D. Nation, *"Education within and without classrooms: Sustaining quality through technological change", In A. Tait, (ed.):* Quality Assurance in Open and Distance Learning—European and International Perspectives, Cambridge: The Open University, 1993.

Filipczak, B., *"Putting the Learning into Distance Learning"*, Training 32. :111-118, October, 1995.

Floor P. (ed.), Beyond Humanities, Long-term Strategy for ODL in University Environments and Virtual Mobility, Brussels, Coimbra Group, 1998.

______________ , *Networked Services for Quality Distance Learning, in* ODL Networking for Quality Learning, in Proceedings of Lisbon 2000 Conference of the European ODL Liaison Committee, Lisbon, 2000.

Foks, J., Open Learning and Distance Education in South Africa: Communications for Learning, University of Pretoria: Bureau for Academic Support Services, 1995.

Garrison, D.R., *"An analysis and evaluation of audio teleconferencing to facilitate education at a distance"*, The American Journal of Distance Education, 4(3), 16-23, 1990.

Hancock, A. Contemporary Information and Communication Technologies and Education. International Commission on Education for the 21 st Century. UNESCO, 1993

Harasim, L. (ed.), Online Education, New York: Praeger, 1990.

Holloway, R.E., and J., Ohler, *"Distance education in the next decade", In G.J. Anglin (ed.),* Instructional technology, Past, Present, and Future, *Englewood, CO:* Libraries Unlimited, 1991, pp. 259-66.

Jenkins, J., S., Inquai, T. Dodds, and D., Warr, *"Distance teaching: A catalyst for curricular change for introducing vocational subjects"*, ERIC document: ED 280984, 1986.

Jonassen, D.H., "Applications and limitations of hypertext technology for distance learning", Paper presented at the Distance Learning Workshop, Armstrong Laboratory, San Antonio, TX, 1992.

Keegan, D., The Foundations of Distance Education, London: Croom Helm, 1986.

Keith, Harry, John Magnus, and Keegan Desmond (eds.), Distance Education: New Perspectives, New York: Routledge Publishers, 1993.

Kell, D., et al., "Educational technology and the restructuring movement: Lessons from research on computers in classrooms", Paper presented at the Annual Meeting of the American Educational Research Association, Boston, 1990.

Kennedy, Paul, Preparing for the 21 st Century, Random House, 1993.

Kerr, E., S., Hiltz, Computer-Based Instruction, *17(1), 1982.*

Lockwood, F. (ed.), Open and Distance Learning Today, London, Routledge.

Lockwood, Fred, ed., Open and Distance Learning Today, London and New York: Routledge Publishing, 1995.

Martin, B. L., *"Using Distance Education to Teach Instructional Design to Preservice Teachers"*, Educational Technology, Vol. XXXIV, No. 3, March 1994.

Miller, G., *"Distance education encounters new technologies"*, American Independent Study Newsletter, Fall, 1993.

_______________ , *"Technology, the curriculum and the learner: Opportunities for open and distance education"*, In R. Mills and A. Tait (eds.), Supporting the learner in open and distance learning, London, Pitman, 1996.

Mills, R. and A. Tait (eds.), Supporting the Learner in Open and Distance Learning, *London, Pitman, 1996.*

Moore, M. G., and G. Kearsley, Distance Education: A Systems View, Belmont, Calif.: Wadsworth Publishing, 1996.

Mukhopadhyay, Marmar and Susan Phillips (eds.), Open Scholing: Selected Experiences, *The Commonwealth of Learning, Vancouver*, 1994.

Nisbet, J., "Issues/Questions", *In* Curricular Reform: Assessment in Question, Paris, OECD, 1993.

Osberg, K. M., *Virtual reality and education: where imagination and experience meet,* VR in the Schools, 1995.

Owston, R.D., *"The World Wide Web, A Technology to Enhance Teaching and Learning?"*, In Educational Researcher, 26, 1997.

Pea, R.A., *"Seeing what we build together: Distributed multimedia learning environments for transformative communications"*, Journal of the Learning Sciences, 3(3), 285-299, 1994.

Perraton, H. (ed.), Distance Education for Teacher Training, London and New York: Routledge, 1993.

Perraton, H. (ed.), Distance Education: An Economic and Educational Assessment of its Potential, World Bank. 1986.

Perraton, H. and C., Creed, Applying new technologies and cost-effective delivery systems in basic education, Paris: UNESCO, 2000 .

Perraton, H., *"A theory for distance education", In D. Sewart, D. Keegan, and B. Holmberg (eds.),* Distance education: International Perspectives, New York: Routledge, 1988, pp. 34-45.

______________ , Open and Distance Learning in the Developing World, London, Routledge, 2000.

Petre, et. al., *"Innovations in Large-Scale Supported Distance Teaching: Transformation for the Internet, Not Just Translation",* Journal of Engineering Education, October 1998.

Portway, P., and C., Lane, Technical Guide to Tele-conferencing and Distance Learning, San Ramon, CA: Applied Business telecommunications, 1992.

Ravitch, D., *"Technology and the curriculum", in M.A. White (ed.),* What curriculum for the information age? Hillsdale, NJ: Lawrence Erlbaum Associates, Inc., 1987.

Rowntree, D., Exploring Open and Distance Learning, London: Kogan Page, 1992.

Rumble, G., The Costs and Economics of Open and Distance Learning, London: Kogan Page, 1997.

Schamber, L., *"Delivery systems for distance education",* ERIC Document Reproduction Service No. ED 304 111, 1988.

Schlosser, C.A., and M.L. Anderson, Distance Education: Review of the Literature, Washington, DC: Association for Educational Communications and Technology, 1994.

Sherry, L S. *"Issues in Distance Learning",* International Journal of Distance Education, vol.1, 1996.

Tait, A., *"Planning Student Support in Open and Distance Learning", in* Open Learning, 15 (3), 287-300, 2000.

______________ , Quality Assurance in Distance Education: International Case Studies, Vancouver: The Commonwealth of Learning, 1997.

Taylor, J.C., *"Distance education technologies: The fourth generation".* Australian Journal of Educational Technology, 11, 2, 1-7, 2000.

UNESCO, Analytical Survey, Distance Education for the Information Society, Policies, Pedagogy and Professional Development, UNESCO Institute for Information Technologies in Education, Moscow: UNESCO/IITE, 2000.

_______________ , Distance Education in the E-9 Countries, The Development and Future of Distance Education Programmes in the Nine High-Population Countries, Paris: UNESCO, 2001.

_______________ , "Learning: the Treasure Within", Report to UNESCO of the International Commission on Education for the Twenty-first Century, Paris: UNESCO, 1996.

_______________ , Teacher Education through Distance Learning, Technology, Curriculum, Evaluation, Cost, Paris: UNESCO, 2001.

_______________ , The Experience of Internet Usage in Education, an Analytical Survey, *UNESCO Institute for Information Technologies in Education (IITE),* Moscow: UNESCO/IITE, 2000.

_______________ , The New Information and Comunication Technologies For the Development of Education, Science and Culture, 161 EX/INF. 12, Paris: UNESCO, 2001.

Williams, M., and K., Paprock, *Instructional design in distance education.* The ED Journal, 7(4), 1994.

Wurster, S., Distance Education: Beneath the Surface, Techtrends, 1996.

Index